The Rise and Fall of Korea's Economic Development

Sung-Hee Jwa

The Rise and Fall of Korea's Economic Development

Lessons for Developing and Developed Economies

palgrave
macmillan

Sung-Hee Jwa
Chairman, Park Chung Hee Memorial Foundation
Seoul, Korea (Republic of)

ISBN 978-3-319-58064-7 ISBN 978-3-319-58065-4 (eBook)
DOI 10.1007/978-3-319-58065-4

Library of Congress Control Number: 2017944171

Printed on acid-free paper

This Palgrave Macmillan imprint is published by Springer Nature
The registered company is Springer International Publishing AG
The registered company address is: Gewerbestrasse 11, 6330 Cham, Switzerland

Preface

The Korean economy has for a long time been a most interesting and controversial area for economic research. Beginning from the 1950s when South Korea was an underdeveloped, agrarian economy that depended heavily on foreign aid, the nation rose at remarkable speed to become a major international economic power, the fourth largest economy in Asia and the 13th largest in the world. Korea's modernization was brought about by Park Chung-hee, who is widely regarded as almost single-handedly having initiated the transformation of the Korean economy through his economic management and policies which I characterize as development policy by "economic discrimination": that is, a meritocratic system based on economic performance that by treating differences differently helps those who help themselves. This economic discrimination paradigm instilled in all Koreans, individuals, villages, and corporations, the "self-help" spirit that allowed them to grow and develop. Specifically, a conducive climate was created that encouraged small- and medium-sized firms to grow into large conglomerates to lead national economic growth through exports and industrialization.

As I write this preface, the impeachment of Park Geun-Hye (daughter of Park Chung-hee) the 18th term President of South Korea who took office in 2013 has taken the country by storm. In between the regimes of father and daughter, Korea's political landscape has changed drastically by which "economic egalitarianism" has substituted "economic discrimination" and has positioned itself at the center of social and political discussions. From "Park to Park"—father to daughter—and all the many episodes in between, this book takes a closer look at Korea through the new General Theory of Economic Development lens tracing its trials and tribulations for over the 60 or so years.

The study of the Korean economic development has so far failed to come under satisfactory scrutiny by mainstream economists largely because Korea during the miracle years adopted heterodox policies that are not fully supported by the mainstream economic schools, as well as world economic organizations like the World Bank and IMF, while the recent experience in the post-miracle years with the introduction of the market economy and political democracy with the hope to transform Korea into a developed economy has thus far turned out to be far less satisfactory than expected.

A central theme of this book is the interpretation of the Korean economy with my General Theory of Economic Development (published by Edward Elgar in 2017) that serves as the analytical framework to better understand the Korean economy. The theory I have proposed goes beyond the market-centric view as well as the contemporary neo-classical models that see Korea's unprecedented rise more of an anomaly than something which can be explained in their model. My theory also goes beyond the pro-government school that looks at Korea's economic miracle as a result of infant-industry protection. Neither interpretations, as I argue in the book, are satisfactory.

Incidentally, almost 15 years back in 2001, I wrote a book titled "A New Paradigm for Korea's Economic Development" which is also published by Palgrave that looked at Korea's future economic reform from the broad market-centric perspective as well as blending in ideas with the New Institutional Economics. That book also looked closely at macroeconomic policy issues as Korea had then been hit by the 1997/98 Asian financial crisis. In contrast, this book I believe goes deeper by applying my General Theory of Economic Development to better understand the Korean economy, as well as looking more thoroughly at institutional factors that have affected Korea's past and current economic evolution, and thereby deriving some important lessons to be learned by developing and developed countries.

The Korean economic story is of course not all rosy, and I carefully dissect and provide reasons for the long-term economic stagnation of the recent decades that have seen a rise in inequality, a slowdown in economic growth, and an overall increasing dissatisfaction of the Korean people with life in general. Ironically, all these economic and social woes have coincided with increased extent of the market economy and political democracy. This book attempts to provide an explanation for this apparent paradox. And by tracing the rise and fall of Korea's economic development, an important purpose of this book is to provide lessons for developing as well as developed countries. What would be the useful lessons that could be learned by developing countries in Africa, Southeast Asia, and Latin America? What are the things to be avoided? What can non-developing developed countries (including Korea) learn about the current economic stagnation? The book hopes to provide answers to these perennial and important questions.

Seoul, Korea (Republic of) Sung-Hee Jwa

Acknowledgement

This book is the outcome of a long period of new thinking about Korea's economic development that has benefited from many people. Some of the material has been used extensively in my teaching about the Korean economy at Seoul National University, Korea Development Institute School of Public Policy, and Yeungnam University, among other institutions. I would like to thank Professor of Economics, Dr. Yong Yoon at Chulalongkorn University in Bangkok for his help with the book beyond extensive English editing. Also, my appreciation goes to the editors and anonymous referees at Palgrave, Dr. Taekyu Lee, an Economist at the Korea Economic Research Institute for working on data and empirical work, and Dr. Taejoon Han, a Senior Fellow at President Park Chung Hee Memorial Foundation in Korea for his English editing and contribution. Finally, my appreciation goes to my family for their encouragement during the long period of working on this book.

Contents

List of Figures

List of Tables

CHAPTER 1

Introduction

Abstract This chapter suggests that both the pro-market and the pro-government views are flawed especially when it comes to understanding and explaining Korea's economy, its challenges, achievements and woes. Despite the recent renewed interest in the economic policies of Park Chung Hee, a consistent understanding of the mechanisms of Korea's economic development is largely absent in the literature. The book essentially fills this gap by interpreting the Korean economy by the author's General Theory of Economic Development (GTED).

Keywords Korean economic development · Park Chung Hee
Pro-market view · Pro-government view

Over the past few decades, Korea's economic development experiences have been documented and studied not only to further our understanding of the complex nature of economic development as a matter of academic interest, but also to search for and learn useful policy lessons for developing economies in Asia, Africa and Latin America. Korea's experiences pose many interesting questions that are not yet satisfactorily answered in a persuasive manner. A number of authors and commentators on Korea provide diverse views on the nature of Korea's developmental experience over the past 60 years, but to the latecomers the spectrum of theories taken together is often contradictory and confusing. The interpretation and theoretical arguments of Korea's experience

S.-H. Jwa, *The Rise and Fall of Korea's Economic Development*,
DOI 10.1007/978-3-319-58065-4_1

stretch too widely such that finding a single useful lesson or policy guideline for the latecomers seems impossible.

Much of the debate on Korea's development is between two camps, the pro-market and the pro-government supporters. The so-called neoclassical economists together with market fundamentalists have often viewed Korea's developmental experience as a kind of anomaly from the standpoint of the free market economy; something unexpected and most likely impossible to replicate.[1] On the other hand, the pro-government industrialization policy camp has emphasized the importance of the government's industrialization policy for Korea's economic development, but their logic tends to be mainly defensive and sometimes not very convincing.[2] Somewhat embarrassingly, there are differences in views by experts on the actual role played by the government in the process of Korea's development. Pro-market supporters can be heard arguing that there was in fact hardly anything important that the government did and dismiss the idea of "government-led development" as a misnomer. They argue that Korea's development was led by market forces and that the government, in fact, may have been a hindrance rather than a complement to economic development. Taken to the extreme, it has been argued that Korea would have achieved even higher economic growth rates than what had actually been achieved if it were not for government intervention.[3] On the other hand, the pro-government supporters usually accepting the notion of government-led development are at the same time unable to divorce themselves from the logic of the free market view, which is reflected in their rather weak and unsatisfactory justification of the need for government intervention. The whole field of development economics as well as the search for a coherent and persuasive explanation of Korea's developmental experience is now seriously in disarray.

Even more embarrassing is the fact that some Korean commentators today have chosen to steer away from the Park Chung Hee economic policy paradigm (whether such a paradigm exists or not will be a discussed later on) ever since the 1980s by declaring Korea's modernization program of the 1960s and 1970s as seriously flawed and misguided. This resenting voice instead advocates a paradigm shift in the opposite direction to Park's intentions and methods to move Korea forward. Casual observation shows, however, that the Korean economy seems not to have performed as well as it did in the Park's era (and the early post-Park era until the late-1980s). Instead, a continuously decaying growth trend since the late-1980s has resulted that is accompanied by many economic woes, now carrying Korea further adrift and away from true development. That notwithstanding, especially since becoming an official overseas development aid nation in 2009, Korea has actively promoted Park's economic paradigm, in various guises and modes, to latecomers around the globe. But there continues to be hardly any consensus about the nature of Korea's take-off and economic development. Consequently, an understanding of Korea's economic development is now more seriously wanting than ever before.

Quo Vadis? Where can latecomers as well as Korea herself look for to find the secret to economic growth and development? This book acts as a pathfinder by applying my new General Theory of Economic Development (Jwa 2017) that explains not only the *condensed* developmental experiences of Korea, as well as China and Japan, but also the *extended* experiences of Western nations. Applying the new framework here should help answer the most pressing and interesting questions about Korea's economic developmental experiences which development economists as well as policymakers in the developing economies will be most anxious to know about.

This book is written in a kind of essay-style. And as such, I have taken enormous liberty to discuss and explore a range of rather subjectively chosen issues about Korea's economic development. The style of writing is also intended to invite curious readers into further discussion and debate. The rest of this book is organized as follows: Chapter 2 looks at some important myths about the Korean economic miracle propagated by mainstream, market-centric and pro-government camps, as well as those that have adhered to the democratic political perspective. I highlight also some of the realities that dismiss such misunderstandings and raise pertinent questions about development economics in general. Chapter 3 provides a brief overview of Development Economics as a discipline highlighting the features of different schools and approaches as well as their limitations in explaining Korea's modernization. Chapter 4 introduces briefly my new General Theory of Economic Development (GTED) which is based on the consolidation of various heterogeneous approaches and diverse experiences that I have explored over the years. Its scope is rather general and wide in the sense that it goes beyond the institutional-free model building economic discussions commonly found in mainstream economics, by taking into account the importance of institutions or "rules of the game"; not only do I discuss formal and informal institutions, but I highlight and acknowledge the importance of the corporate firm in economic development. Chapter 5 is an overview of developmental experiences around the world over time by applying my new theory of economic development. Chapter 6 focuses on the economic development history of Korea over the past 60 years. In this chapter, I will clarify the reasons why Korea's economic performances turn out to be so radically different over the past 60 years with a turning point in the late-1980s. Chapter 7 I hope will provide the main value-added for readers in developing as well as developing countries as I explain the eight most important lessons from Korea's economic development related to the question "How did Korea become so successful and then later experience economic growth stagnation and decline?" Chapter 8 discusses the reproducibility of the Korean economic miracle. The book ends with Chap. 9 which briefly concludes by consolidating the key lessons of the book.

Notes

1. World Bank (1993).
2. Rodrick (2011).
3. Sakong and Koh (2010).

References

Jwa, Sung-Hee. 2017. *A General Theory of Economic Development: Towards A Capitalist Manifesto.* Cheltenham: Edward Elgar.

Rodrik, Dani. 2011. "Perspectives on the New Industrial Policy" a PPT Presentation at the International Conference on Rethinking Industrial Policy in the Era of Global Socio-Economic Restructuring, Organized by Korea Institute for Industrial Economics and Trade, in Seoul, December.

Sakong, Il, and Youngsun Koh (eds.). 2010. *The Korean Economy: Six Decades of Growth and Development, The Committee for the 60-years History of Korean Economy.* Seoul: Korea Development Institute.

World Bank. 1993. *The East Asian Miracle: Economic Growth and Public Policy.* New York: Oxford University Press.

CHAPTER 2

Myths and Realities of Korea's Economic Development

Abstract This chapter discusses four negative myths about Korea in the 1960s and 1970s, namely, that Park Chung Hee's regime (1) was anti-liberal, anti-democratic, and anti-free market, (2) was characterized by strong, government-led industrial policies that directly distorted and intervened in the market, (3) created monopolies which encouraged the concentration of economic power in large corporations with the pro-chaebol corporate policies, and (4) created unbalanced regional, sectoral, and corporate development. By arguing that these myths are largely unfounded, the chapter spells out the motivation and aims of the book.

Keywords Policy regime of Park Chung Hee · Anti-Park Chung Hee Government-led industrial policy · Concentration of economic power Unbalanced development

Korea under Park Chung Hee's leadership during her take-off and developmental era in the 1960s and 1970s are full of examples of numerous unorthodox policies that would not sit comfortably with mainstream economics or political ideology. Korea's economic achievements continue to remain controversial, clouded with many myths and confusion created among domestic as well as international commentators and scholars. We begin by outlining some of the myths and realities about Park's national management and economic policies.

S.-H. Jwa, *The Rise and Fall of Korea's Economic Development*,
DOI 10.1007/978-3-319-58065-4_2

Myths on Park's Economic Development Policy Paradigm

Myth One: Park's non-democratic, authoritarian leadership should have been detrimental to Korea's economic development because such a regime is anti-liberal, anti-democratic, and anti-free market. As such, Park's economic as well as political regime is not to be recommended to nor replicated by other latecomers and developing economies. Korea also should abandon Park's way of economic management if there is any hope for further development. In fact, the later Korean governments all made concerted efforts to dismantle Park's economic policies as well as his political regime. The verdict: Korea is described as a country that has embraced fully the notion and practice of political democracy and market economy albeit with disappointing economic results.

Myth Two: Park's economic policy regime adopted strong, government-led industrial policies by directly intervening in the market place and therefore, cannot be a successful benchmark for other developing economies. In fact, Korea's industrial policies were initially not endorsed by the World Bank ever since their initiation and were officially declared a failure by the Korean government in the early 1980s. Furthermore, there appears to be a consensus that Park's industrial policy should not be repeated if true development is to be achieved. As such, Korea's industrial policy regime since the 1980s has turned into a regime of functional support policies, instead of being aimed at certain industries or firms.

Myth Three: Park's economic policy regime created concentration of economic power by promoting large corporations through adopting a pro-chaebol corporate policy, which enhanced monopoly power as well as help deepen politics-and-business interlocking that became a source of widespread corruption. The post-Park consensus concludes that Park's regime was largely against the free and competitive market principles and therefore the economic power of the chaebol should be dismantled and their investment activities for any further expansion should be tightly controlled. Korea according to this anti-chaebol consensus has adopted a systematic set of regulatory policies putting a grip on the large corporations' investment as well as management activities, while on the other hand adopting a strong Small-and-Medium-Sized Enterprise (SME) support system that hopes to establish a balanced corporate ecosystem and a competitive market economy.

Myth Four: As a way of summary, Park's regime is said to have created unbalanced regional, sectoral, and corporate development. This is seen as incompatible with balanced development, which has been proposed by some authors and most political leaders as a fundamental feature of a developed economy. Therefore, for the last 30 years, adopting a development path exactly opposite of Park's is regarded as the way forward towards a developed economy.

Realities and Pertinent Queries on Economic Development

Reality One: The above myths notwithstanding, Korea's fastest growth and the best shared growth experience of 30 years, which is also confirmed by the World Bank (1993) and perhaps unprecedented in human history, is associated with Park's political authoritarianism and economic interventionist policy.

Reality Two: In spite of the "failure of Korea's industrial policy," the very conglomerates that grew under the Heavy and Chemical Industry (HCI) promotion policy, which never found favor in mainstream economics, have continued to lead the Korean Economy. This is a strong counter-evidence against Myth two and three above, implying that Park's industrial policy may in fact have been indispensable to Korea's development and that the large corporations are not the "evil monster" working against national interest as some of us are made to believe.

Reality Three: The Korean Economy currently suffers from low growth and worsening inequality despite the past three decades of drastic policy shift that "corrects" the alleged misguided Park's paradigm to further push Korea towards an advanced economy.

Quo Vadis? Given the huge rift between the myths and the realities, one cannot but feel embarrassed and intrigued with the state of the art in development economics, i.e. its failure to explain the Korean economic development experiences. Perhaps there is good reason to be suspicious about the validity of existing perspectives on economic development. In this context, some observations about the realities of Korea's development could help clarify some pressing and pertinent queries on the development process in general.

First, it is interesting to ask how many examples in history there are of economic catch-up of nations that had adopted the Western style one-man-one vote democratic political system before development or with the market alone? The answer: Not many or only a few at best.[1] This book hopes to shed some light on why this is the case.

Second, despite strong historical evidence of successful industrial policies of countries like Korea, Japan and China, it is important to ask now whether industrial policy should be disregarded as is often argued in mainstream textbooks. This book hopes to provide a convincing alternative framework to such mainstream thinking as well as to supplement the somewhat weak existing pro-industrial policy argument. Moreover, should economists continue to preach that markets will take care of most things regarding development? Should economics as a respectable discipline continue to dwell on the "all or nothing" debate on the role of government versus the market? Be that as it may, controversy is everywhere and policy makers in developing economies remain confused.

Third, it remains puzzling whether it is possible to achieve economic development without such features as "economic concentration" in favor of growing corporations and regions, and "unbalanced development." This book will explain why this is impossible, and that in fact, such features are necessary features of development for growing economies. Development without differences and inequalities based on the ideology of equality and balance appears to have become the modern view of economic progress among us. This book will argue that such kind of development is simply a mirage. This is akin to tying your own hands so as not to allow one to select and choose, or "economically discriminate" based on economic performances in the market place. We seem to forget too easily that our selection instincts are intrinsically and fundamentally inseparable with economic development and with all those unequal outcomes in the market.

Fourth, this book aims to find lessons for developing and developed economies as well as for Development Economics (as a subject) from Korea's experiences which we split into two drastically different periods: the era of successful "misguided" Park's paradigm and the democratized and market-centric but failing mainstream economic policy paradigm in the post-Park era. The later chapters intend to explain the reason for such dichotomy of economic performances and to draw some key lessons by utilizing my new General Theory of Economic Development (Jwa 2017). Having explained in Chap. 6 such uncomfortable realities of Korean economic development, Chap. 7 highlights the eight most useful lessons for developing as well as developed economies following Korea's experiences which will help clarify some of the myths and queries about economic development.

Note

1. Note that Mercantilism could be reinterpreted as a precursor for Industrial Revolution and most of the now developed economies had infant industry protection policies under a relatively non-democratic political regime during the early part of their industrial revolution. See Chang (2002) for similar view.

References

Chang, Ha-Joon. 2002. *Kicking away the Ladder: Development Strategy in Historical Perspective*. London: Anthem Press.

Jwa, Sung-Hee. 2017. *A General Theory of Economic Development: Towards A Capitalist Manifesto*. Cheltenham: Edward Elgar.

World Bank. 1993. *The East Asian Miracle: Economic Growth and Public Policy*. New York: Oxford University Press.

CHAPTER 3

A Brief Overview of Economic Development Theories

Abstract This chapter provides a critique of economic development theories starting from Adam Smith to the "capital-injection" school (Harrod-Domar, Lewis and Rostow models), the neo-classical growth models (Solow and Romer models) and the so-called Washington consensus. Furthermore, by taking a closer look at more specific arguments on the Korean economy such as Amsden's revisionist approach, the World Bank's view and Chang Ha-Joon's infant industry argument, this chapter exposes the various weaknesses of these theories in explaining Korea's economic development experiences.

Keywords Economic development theories · Capital-injection school Neo-classical growth models · Revisionist · Infant industry argument Washington consensus · Egalitarianism

Adam Smith in his "Wealth of Nations" (1776) writes that the "division of labor is limited by the extent of the market." That is, from the supply side of the economy, given the stock of capital, labor and other resources, Smith championed the division of labor as the key factor behind building the capacity to produce economic value and wealth. The division of labor or specialization was the main "technological aspect" driving economic development. That is, economies of scale were said to

S.-H. Jwa, *The Rise and Fall of Korea's Economic Development*,
DOI 10.1007/978-3-319-58065-4_3

be realized through the division of labor, and specialization was hence the main source of wealth creation or economic development. And regarding the demand side of the economy, Smith argued that the extent of the market constrained the scale of production, which gave rise to the proposition that trade (based on *laissez faire*) is an important determinant of economic development. It is difficult to criticize Smith given his great contribution to economics, but it is worth mentioning here that he was essentially a champion of liberalism, a product of his times, and as such, was allergic to any form of elitism or concentration of economic power. In this sense, he completely failed to see the importance of conglomerations for the development of the capitalist economy as can be seen from his overly critical view of the role of large corporation in his *Wealth of Nations*.[1]

Be that as it may, development economics as a separate discipline can be traced only recently to the period after the Second World War when economists turned to address the need for, and likely problems with, the industrialization of Eastern Europe.[2] Only after the 1950s did economists turn their attention towards Asia, Africa and Latin America. At the heart of these studies, economists such as Simon Kuznets and W. Arthur Lewis looked not only at economic growth but also structural transformation. The history of development economics is a fascinating and interesting one, which I can only discuss briefly in this chapter mainly to highlight some important features, limitations and controversies.

The Early "Capital-Injection" Developmental Schools

The Harrod-Domar model, an early post-Keynesian model of economic growth, was used in development economics to explain an economy's growth rate in terms of the level of saving and productivity of capital. Essentially Harrod (1939) and Domar (1946) proposed that a country's growth rate was proportional to the share of investment spending. Despite government efforts to encourage savings (to increase investment) the difference between the required investment and the country's own savings, referred to as the financing gap, was usually assumed to be substantial in less developed economies, therefore warranting the need for donors from more advanced countries to step in and transfer capital stock (aid) to developing countries to help increase their productive capacity needed to attain targeted growth. Beyond the technical simplicity in explaining growth dynamics and various criticisms about assumptions made regarding, for example, its failure to acknowledge the diminishing returns of capital, changing labor productivity, and technological improvements, the Harrod-Domar model has very little if anything at all to say about development strategy: the actual implementation of policy to achieve targeted developmental goals.

Similarly, in the same vein as Harrod and Domar, the Nobel Economics Laureate W. Arthur Lewis in the 1950s argued that capital or machines were the binding constraints on production, stating explicitly that, "the central fact of economic development is rapid capital accumulation."[3] In the 1960s, a prominent American development economist W.W. Rostow (1960) argued that economic modernization occurs in five basic stages of varying length: traditional society, preconditions for take-off, take-off, drive to maturity, and high mass consumption. He further stressed that an increase in the investment rate (from 5 to 10%) was necessary for the essential "take-off" stage for sustained growth.

How does the financing gap approach face up against actual experience? Easterly (2002, pp. 37–38) shows that only 17 out of 88 countries between 1965 to 1995 showed positive statistical association between aid and investment, and just 6 of the 17 countries showed that investment increased at least one for one with aid. Broadly speaking, the capital-injection approach failed because it did not tie policy to incentives. There is no reason to think that aid provided to poorer recipient countries, for example, would automatically change incentives to invest in the future. That is, capital transfer does not automatically increase investment, but rather, has been used to increase the purchase of consumption goods.

The Neo-classical Growth Models

Robert M. Solow, an American economist and recipient of the John Bates Clark Medal (1961) and the Nobel Memorial Prize in Economic Sciences (1987), together with Trevor Swan in 1956 developed the so-called Solow growth model as an extension of the Harrod-Domar Model. It is a "growth accounting" production function model stating that three factors—technology, capital accumulation and the labor force—drive economic growth. Although increasing capital accumulation and the labor force may increase economic growth, the Solow growth model does not view capital injection as a source of growth in the long run because of diminishing returns: the returns to each additional machine will become lower and lower as one adds more and more machines relative to workers. This also implies that saving (deferred consumption, which makes up investment) does not contribute to long-run growth.

Solow's "solution" to this riddle was to introduce the idea of "technology change". That is, once the steady-state is reached and the resources in a country are used up, economic growth rate can only be increased through innovation and improvements in technology. One can think of technology as a kind of blueprint that arranges workers and machines in more efficient ways. Hence, technological change would mean improvement in such blueprints. Be that as it may, the same conclusion arises: additional capital or machinery per worker cannot be a source of long-run growth, but only helps along with the transition to the long-run path. Furthermore, because poor countries have less capital to start with, and as such each additional unit of capital will have a higher return than in a rich country, the Solow model predicts that the gap between rich and poor countries will narrow, a concept called convergence. Whether we have convergence or not remains controversial. Summers and Heston (1987) for example showed that poor countries were not growing any faster than the rich ones during the Cold War era, while Barro (1997) finds evidence to support convergence.

Having put forward the idea that technological progress dictates economic growth, a major criticism of the Solow model is that it does not treat the causative factors of technological progress, leaving it as an exogenous factor in the growth process. That is, technological progress in the model is determined by non-economic causes like advancement in the basic sciences. It thus ignores the problems of inducing technical progress through the process of learning, investment in research, and capital accumulation. This is the challenge taken up by a number of researchers in the 1990s, especially Paul Romer in 1990, who took up the task of finding out what kinds of economic factors actually govern technological advance.

In general, the so-called AK models or endogenous growth models, linked improvements in productivity to faster pace of innovation and investment in human capital. Indeed, positive externalities and spillover effects from high-value added knowledge economies are treated as sources of competitiveness and higher rates of innovation. It is therefore not surprising that proponents of these models stress the importance of educating people, subsidizing research, and importing ideas from abroad. It also carefully gauges the protection offered to intellectual property, i.e. beefing up the country's research and development (R&D) sector. It is worth mentioning that innovation has been a central subject of not only the Neo-classical growth thinkers but also of Schumpeter, who is famous for his "creative destruction" concept, which highlights the fact that economies progress as old technologies are replaced by newer ones (e.g., typewriters replaced by modern word processors.) Moreover, the importance of "human capital" is also acknowledged by Gary Becker (1964). Education (as an investment in human capital) is then seen as an engine of economic development. Nevertheless, several studies have failed to find a strong empirical association between education (years of schooling) and GDP growth. The weak empirical support for education as a factor of economic development, however, may be due to confounding.

It is important to note here that the endogenous growth approach does recognize a positive role of the government in correcting potential market failures stemming from externalities and economies of scale, protection of intellectual property rights, and promotion of R&D policies. More generally, however, it does not advocate "direct" government intervention, such as promoting corporations, as is discussed later, probably due to its preoccupation with the market equilibrium framework. Moreover, despite its importance, technology is not a panacea for growth, nor will it translate automatically into economic development if the incentives for creating as well as using it are absent or not strong enough. Indeed, incentives related to innovation are very complex. More problematically, innovators cannot capture all of the returns to their innovation because of imitation and free-riding. Although, as we have repeatedly mentioned elsewhere (Jwa 2017) positive externalities are part and parcel of the economic development matrix, and they must be identified and targeted so that resources are properly channeled or "internalized". The essential question for economic development is then: how and by whom? By its nature, the market by itself mostly fails to internalize important externalities, especially in the presence of high transaction costs, so the textbook answer would typically be some form of government support or action. But this neglects to explicitly recognize the essential role of a third actor, namely, the corporate firm. The government's action to internalize positive externalities may provide the fundamental incentives for innovation, but without the organizational skills and support of the corporate firm, it would be difficult if not impossible for innovation to become reality in an imperfectly competitive marketplace. It is one of the main theoretical contentions of this book that as much as the government, the role of the corporate firm as a private organization is absolutely essential and indispensable to a nation's economic growth and development by supplementing the market failure.[4]

I will continue this discussion in the following chapter with the story of the New Institutional Economics (NIE) that shifted economic analysis away from institution-free models by considering institutions or "rules of the game" to explain how they may shape economic development.

Washington Consensus and Egalitarianism

Having discussed the functional approaches to development under the neoclassical tradition, we need to look further at a rather popular development policy paradigms. In line with market-centric as well as neoliberal view, over the last 30 some years, the so-called "Washington Consensus," a collective list of policy items from various theoretical approaches, has been proposed as one of the most popular developmental policy reform packages for developing countries.[5] The Washington Consensus mainly involves advocating the provision of private property rights (PPR) and economic freedom (EF), together with improvement in education, research and development (R&D), the rule of law, a nation's social overhead capital (SOC), and macroeconomic stability. All along, the list of policy items in the Washington consensus has grown to include various policy ideas as new approaches and needs arise. However, today the contribution of the Washington Consensus is in serious question mostly because it has largely failed to fully take account of the nature of underdevelopment by mainly propagating market-centric policy suggestions.

In addition, in the post-WWII era, widespread egalitarianism has sought economic equality as a goal as well as a precondition for economic development. In fact, this has led to so-called revised capitalism that accommodates social democracy, which today has become the political economy norm in many places around the world. The surprising and unexpected outcome, however, is that most of the very economies that have embraced market democracy are now confronted with growth stagnation and income polarization. The need to have a convincing alternative development theory as well as policy paradigms has become more urgent than ever.

We will now conclude this chapter with a short discussion of some interesting commentaries of Korea's developmental experience.

Explaining Korea's Miracle Growth

Markets? Government? Savings? Capital? Education? Exports? Indeed what factor(s) brought about Korea's economic miracle? Is there a "single" explanation or was it all just luck? Can Korea's experience be replicated in other countries? These questions are as plenty as they are pressing.

The World Bank (1993) largely credited neoliberal policies including maintenance of export-led regimes, low taxes, and minimal welfare states that encouraged market principles, for Korea's economic "miracle". This view is not without its critics. Many have argued that the industrial policies of Korea and other East Asian countries had a much greater influence than the World Bank report suggests. The World Bank report itself acknowledged benefits from policies of financial sector repression, such as preferential low interest rates for loans to specific exporting industries. Many other writers before such as Jagdish Bhagwati, Anne Krueger, Ian Little, and Bela Balassa have taken the view that outward orientation and pro-market policies were the primary forces behind the stellar performance of the once rapidly growing economies such as Korea. More recently, Studwell (2013) explains that Korea's policy was based on the notion of "export discipline," or the provision of subsidies based on export performance, and gives further credit to farmland tenure system reform and financial repression. Alice Amsden's "The Next Giant" (1989) contains a revisionist view of Korea's development by which she argues that relative prices were in fact deliberately distorted to promote investment in order to internalize static and dynamic externalities. Amsden writes that, "…not only has Korea not gotten relative prices right, it has deliberately gotten them 'wrong',"[6] adding that such policy succeeded because of the strong relationship between the government and corporations whereby the government exacted certain performance standards in return for preferential treatment and support. Dani Rodrik (2011) and Robert Wade (2012), too, considers industrial policy to be central to the Korean success and somewhat downplays the role of outward orientation.

Other writers provide different explanations and emphasis, while still others are quick to dismiss that there was a "miracle" at all. Pack and Westphal (1986), for example, also recognizes the importance of outward orientation but assigns a more substantial role to industrial policy, especially in affecting technological changes in selected industries and attributes Korea's economic development to well-trained technocrats with economic expertise working in the ministries in the 1960s that were largely divorced from politics. Alwyn Young (1995), on the other hand, shows empirically that growth in the East Asian NICs including Korea's was mainly due to factor accumulation, with little technical change or total factor productivity growth, thereby spurring the famous controversy in the East Asian "miracle" growth literature.

Of course, there are arguments by Korean authors too, regarding Korea's economic development. Ha-Joon Chang for example stresses the importance of the government, particularly through the so-called "infant industry argument". However, he falls short in his arguments by not providing the constituents of successful government intervention. Similar to Il Sakong and Youngsun Koh (2010), Junho Yoo stresses the importance of the market and even goes as far as arguing that Korea could have attained higher growth rates (more than 10% per annum registered for 18 years) were it not for government intervention. Wonhyuck Lim suggests that the relationships between governments and corporations through the socialization of corporate risk were critical. In a similar vein, Sangwoo Nam argues that relationship of the government and corporations (especially the efficient internal markets of the chaebol) were instrumental.

Most Korean commentators have been overly influenced either by mainstream neoclassical economics with a market-centric, outward orientation view or by the tautological growth accounting framework. Some are attached to a leftist arguments denouncing the value of the miracle itself due to the Park Chung Hee's authoritarian political regime. These views, I contend, are seriously out of the touch with facts and reality.[7]

There seems to be too many characteristics of development in general as well as in Korea-specific context that are left unhandled and unexplained by current theories, and this is why I have over the years developed what I call the General Theory of Economic Development (GTED).[8] My new economic development theory will help reconcile the perennial puzzles of Korea's development laid out in Chap. 2 as myths and realities, providing explanations beyond existing paradigms which cannot satisfactorily explain the Korean case. My theory also deals with many aspects of economic development worldwide as well as in the

Korean context, including for example, political democracy and development, ideology and development, markets versus governments, the role of corporations, economic concentration and conglomeration, success of export strategies as well as heavy and chemical industry promotion policy (HCI drive), and the success of Saemaul Undong (Korea's rural development movement). I also demonstrate why Korea and other nations now face economic stagnation and in some cases decline following many years of modernization. I will use my general theory to explain Korea's economic development—both its rise and its fall—by providing insights into the fundamental causes of economic development. The next chapter introduces the main essence of the new developmental economics theory.

Notes

1. See Chap. 1, Book V in Smith (1776).
2. The key authors at the time were Paul Rosenstein-Rodan, Kurt Mandelbaum and Ragnar Nurkse (see Meier and Seers 1984).
3. Lewis (1954, p. 151).
4. Emphasizing the role of organization beyond market in this book is consistent with Simon's view of the economy as essentially an organizational and not a market economy (Simon 1991).
5. The term "Washington Consensus" was coined by John Williamson (1990) to describe a set of ten relatively specific economic policy prescriptions that he considered constituted the "standard" reform package for developing countries by Washington, DC-based institutions such as the International Monetary Fund (IMF), World Bank, and the US Treasury Department. Wade (2012) has an interesting discussion on how the Washington consensus was formed and how it came to overtake the structural development economics paradigm in recent decades.
6. Amsden (1989, p. 139)
7. Most would argue that Korea's unprecedented growth in the 1960s and 1970s under President Park Chung Hee's regime was unusual and is hard to be explained by the existing theories. Sometimes it is also argued that there is no merit nor is it worthwhile for serious theoretical discussion or investigation because his regime was non-democratic and authoritarian. Most Korean political economists are used to denouncing Park Chung Hee's economic success due to his authoritarianism with an exception of Kim (2004).
8. For a full treatment of the new General Theory of Economic Development, see Jwa (2017), which is a culmination of work from Jwa and Yoon (2004a, b, 2011), Jwa (2008, 2012, 2015).

References

Amsden, Alice. 1989. *Asia's Next Giant: South Korea and Late Industrialization*. New York: Oxford University Press.

Barro, Robert. 1997. *Determinants of Economic Growth: A Cross-Country Empirical Study*. Cambridge, MA: The MIT Press.

Becker, Garry. 1964. *Human Capital: A Theoretical and Empirical Analysis, with Special Reference to Education*. New York: Columbia University Press.

Domar, Evsey. 1946. Capital Expansion, Rate of Growth, and Employment. *Econometrica* 14 (2): 137–147.

Easterly, William. 2002. *The Elusive Quest for Growth: Economists' Adventures and Misadventures in the Tropics*. Cambridge, MA: MIT Press.

Harrod, Roy F. 1939. An Esssay in Dynamic Theory. *The Economic Journal* 49 (193): 14–33.

Jwa, Sung-Hee. 2008. *A New Paradigm of Development Economics: Economic Discrimination Beyond Evolution (In Korean)*. Seoul: Yulgok Publishers Co.

Jwa, Sung-Hee. 2012. *Philosophical Basis for Economic Development (In Korean)*. Seoul: Seoul National University Press.

Jwa, Sung-Hee. 2015. *Park Chung Hee, A Living Economics (In Korean)*. Seoul: Baeknyundongan.

Jwa, Sung-Hee. 2017. *A General Theory of Economic Development: Towards A Capitalist Manifesto*. Cheltenham: Edward Elgar.

Jwa, Sung-Hee, and Yong Yoon. 2004a. Political Institutions and Economic Development: A Study in Economic Discrimination and Political Philosophy. *Seoul Journal of Economics* 17 (3) Fall: 275–307.

Jwa, Sung-Hee, and Yong Yoon. 2004b. A New Look at Development Economics through Korea's Experience: The Paradox of Economic Development. Paper Presented at the 2004 KDI-KAEA Conference, Seoul.

Jwa, Sung-Hee, and Yong Yoon. 2011. Economic Development and Institutions. In *Institutions and National Competitiveness* ed. Young B. Choi. London: Routledge and Kegan Paul.

Kim, Hyung-A. 2004. *Korea's Development Under Park Chung Hee: Rapid Industrialization, 1961–1979*. London: Routledge Cruzon.

Lewis, Arthur. 1954. Economic Development with Unlimited Supplies of Labor. *Manchester School of Economics and Social Studies* 22 (May): 139–191.

Meier, G.M., and D. Seers (eds.). 1984. *Pioneers in Development*. New York: Oxford University Press for the World Bank.

Pack, Howard, and Larry E. Westphal. 1986. Industrial Strategy and Technological Change: Theory Versus Reality. *Journal of Development Economics* 22 (1) (June): 87–128.

Rodrik, Dani. 2011. "Perspectives on the New Industrial Policy" a PPT Presentation at the International Conference on Rethinking Industrial Policy

in the Era of Global Socio-Economic Restructuring, Organized by Korea Institute for Industrial Economics and Trade, in Seoul, December.
Rostow, W.W. 1960. *The Stages of Economic Growth: A Non-Communist Manifesto*. Cambridge, MA: Cambridge University Press.
Sakong, Il, and Youngsun Koh (eds.). 2010. *The Korean Economy: Six Decades of Growth and Development, The Committee for the 60-years History of Korean Economy*. Seoul: Korea Development Institute.
Simon, Herbert A. 1991. Organization and Market. *Journal of Economic Perspectives* 5 (2): 25–44.
Smith, Adam. 1976 [1776]. *An Inquiry into the Nature and Causes of The Wealth of Nation* [Wealth of Nation], ed. Edwin Cannan. Chicago: The University of Chicago Press.
Studwell, Joe. 2013. *How Asia Works: Success and Failure In The World's Most Dynamic Region*. London: Grove Press.
Wade, Robert H. 2012. Return of Industrial Policy? *International Review of Applied Economics* 26 (2): 175–191.
Williamson, John. 1990. What Washington Means by Policy Reform. In *Latin American Readjustment: How Much has Happened*, ed. John Williamson, 7–20. Washington: Institute for International Economics.
World Bank. 1993. *The East Asian Miracle: Economic Growth and Public Policy*. New York: Oxford University Press.
Young, Alwyn. 1995. The Tyranny of Numbers: Confronting the Statistical Realities of the East Asian Growth Experience. *Quarterly Journal of Economics* 110 (August): 641–680.

CHAPTER 4

Pathway to a New Theory of Economic Development

Abstract This chapter summarizes the new General Theory of Economic Development (Jwa 2017) which is adopted to re-interpret Korea's economic development evolution. The importance of viewing the market economy as an economic institution is stressed and a detailed picture of the constitution of a market economy that allows for a more realistic treatment of the economy over the typical institution-free textbook models is provided. Also mentioned is political leadership, including its nature and quality and the prevailing political ideology, as the most important institution guiding the evolution of a society. The author also lays down the essence of the new General Theory of Economic Development based on the idea of "economic discrimination" which is then employed to understand the role of market, especially the importance and relevance of free-riding (i.e. externalities) and the nature of the complex economy, as well as the role of corporate organizations and the government in economic development. It is argued that the key to economic development is the "holy trinity of economic development" which incorporates the market, corporations and the government working in tandem under the principle of economic discrimination.

Keywords General theory of economic development
Economic discrimination · New institutional economics
Corporate economy · Free-riding · Development failure
Holy trinity of economic development · Egalitarianism

S.-H. Jwa, *The Rise and Fall of Korea's Economic Development*,
DOI 10.1007/978-3-319-58065-4_4

In Search for a New Theory of Economic Development

In this chapter, I introduce a new theoretical framework of economic development based on an interpretation of the economy as a complex system, using the evolutionary view of economic change and ideas from the New Institutional Economics (NIE) perspective. Thus far, as I have hinted in the previous chapter, development economics as a discipline has failed to provide a comprehensive, convincing theory of development that can explain not only the western experience but also that of the Northeast Asian countries. In particular, the Korean as well as Chinese economic development is still considered somewhat of an exception according to mainstream theory.

As I have argued, economics can still be said to lack a convincing theory of wealth creation, or a general economic development theory. In this regard, it is interesting to ask how many underdeveloped economies have actually caught up with developed economies in the modern era. How many have achieved visible and sustainable economic development in the past century? Moreover, how many developed economies have been able to maintain stable economic growth and dynamism as well? A quick answer to the above questions is, "Only a very few", despite the fact that economics continues to enjoy the status of a science eligible for the Nobel Prize with increasingly technical elaboration. Hence there is an urgent need to improve economics as a discipline, to find an alternative approach to understanding economic development beyond the prevailing paradigms of the neoclassical growth model and the Washington consensus as well as the egalitarianism.

Dissatisfied with the existing economic development theories, I have developed fully in Jwa (2017) an alternative theory of economic development by incorporating new insights from the New Institutional Economics and Complexity Economics, and my own interpretation of the development process that is consistent with the *extended* Western and *condensed* Northeast Asian economic development experiences. A brief introduction of the main arguments of my alternative approach is presented here.

The Market Economy as an Economic Institution

Nature of Economic Institutions

At the onset, following the New Institutional Economics (NIE) perspective, we begin by defining a market economy as a venue for the economic interaction of individual economic agents under a collection of economic institutions: i.e. an arena where market participants interact under constraints or the "rules of the game," essentially competing or cooperating with one another in pursuit of their individual goals. Each unit strives towards their own survival and success. The rules of the game in the market are defined by economic institutions. Figure 4.1 below describes the market economy as consisting of different layers of sub-economic systems where the outer layers acts as a constraint on inner layers. The market economy can be regarded as an institution-free economy typically depicted in economic textbooks devoid of corporate organizations if only the most inner layer consisting of individuals is considered. For a more

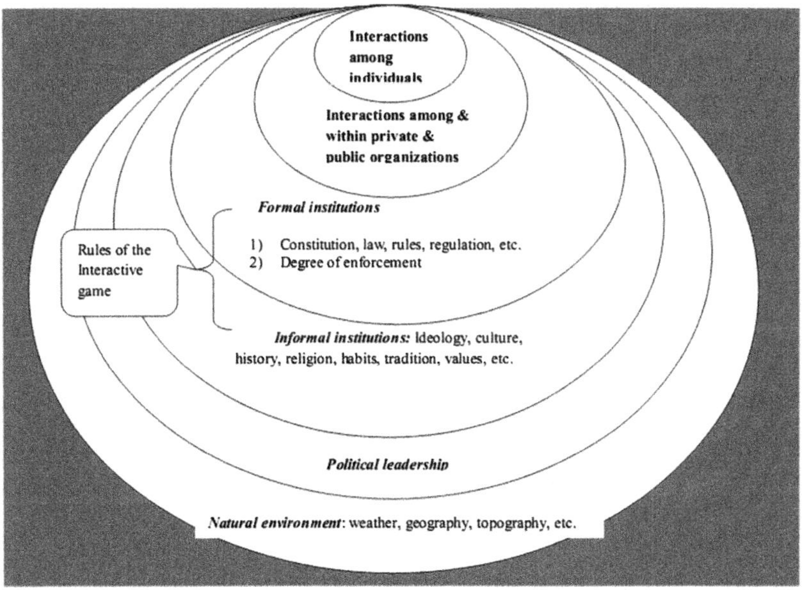

Fig. 4.1 Constitution of market economy. *Source* Jwa (2017)

realistic sub-economy we can consider the organization in the second layer as the most direct constraint on individual behavior. Moving further on, the third layer acts as a constraint on the behaviors of individuals as well as organizations, giving what we would consider as the real market economy driven by formal as well as informal market institutions. Finally, if political leadership (leading the government) in the fourth layer is added to this picture as the ultimate exogenous "rule-setter" and then the physical environment as the ultimate natural constraints, we end with the full-scale modern market economy which constitutes the national economy.

As depicted in Fig. 4.1, it is useful to distinguish between informal and formal institutions, as well as the degree of enforcement of such institutions. Informal institutions consist of informal constraints, such as ideology, history, social norms, cultural environments, and traditional ethics. More often than not, informal institutions help mold the country's legal system. That is, ideology and social norms are often translated into formal institutions such as the constitution (law and order) through the political process. Formal institutions are the written legal constraints on people's economic behavior. Many of today's formal legal institutions have been much influenced by prevailing ideologies that mold the ideology of the ruling political party in the country's rule-making body, and this is even more so in a democratic political regime. In this sense, a country's formal institution is itself constrained by the ideology and social norms prevalent in that society.

However, the causation from informal to formal institutions is increasingly bidirectional since many countries are now introducing as a part of their economic reform package new formal institutions which do not originate from existing informal institutions. These new institutions are said to be development-friendly and to meet the global standard advised by international organizations. In this case, the new formal institutions can act as a new constraint on peoples' behavior which in turn is expected to influence peoples' mindset and ideology, social norm and even culture over the long evolutionary process of institutional change. It turns out that the adoption of such institutional reform depends critically on the political leadership of the country.

The degree of enforcement refers to how strictly formal institutions are enforced, in particular, the law and order of the country imposed on members of the society. Enforcement of formal institutions as well as the binding of informal institutions is important since the mere nominal presence of any institutions (formal or informal) per se does not guarantee any impact on the behavior of people if not strictly enforced or binding.

Therefore, the characteristics of formal and informal institutions, as well as the degree of enforcement of existing institutions in the real world, help transform the textbook model of markets, which often are devoid of real institutions, into a realistic model for understanding real phenomena. For this reason, it is convenient to define the market as one regulated by formal and informal institutions, as well as their intensity of enforcement.[1]

Political Leadership as Exogenous Determinant of Institutions

More importantly, overriding all elements of the institutional environment, or what we might say is the most important institution, is political leadership, including its nature and quality. This is because the political leader(s) play a decisive role in the functioning of formal institutions and thereby influence the nation's socioeconomic behavior as well as informal institutions including ideology, mindset and even the culture, which is in fact the process that one can expect from government-led institutional reforms. In this way, political leadership can directly influence formal institutions and behavior and indirectly affect informal institutions. The leadership thus becomes an independent determinant of the whole society's institutions and economic behaviors (See Fig. 4.1) while in principle, the democratic society's prevailing ideology and mindset influence the political decision via the election process. Political leaders try to follow and/or change ideology and mindset for the purpose of vote maximization, through which process the political leadership becomes, on the one hand, endogenous variable given the existing institutions while, on the other hand, exogenous determinant that create new institutions.

Therefore, the developmental nature and quality of the political leadership as an exogenous determinant of institutions becomes a fundamental precondition for economic growth and development. This is especially true when a country has been "stuck" in an old development-unfriendly trap due to path-dependence and inertia of old institutions such as culture, history, and tradition. The role of the development-friendly political leadership can be essential to steering behavior toward becoming development-friendly. The alternative leadership that seeks to get elected by only following or even reinforcing prevailing development-unfriendly institutions can be called a development-unfriendly-populist.

In fact, the development-friendly nature of market institutions are all derivatives of the quality of national and political leadership, i.e. whether the leadership is development-friendly or not. This issue of development-friendliness of institutions as well as political leadership is the main question to be addressed in this chapter and will accordingly be given full discussion in the following sections.

Ideology is a Key Determinant of Market Institutions and Economic Performances of a National Economy

Institutions or the rules of the game work as constraints on the behavior of economic agents, and thereby influence the economic outcomes of the society. It follows therefore that individuals and organizations have strong incentives to try to change the rules of the game in their favor. A nation's political process is a mechanism often used by the members of a society to influence the rules of the game in their favor, and indeed, political parties and their leaders play a vital role in this process. This is the important reason why we need to emphasize that the rules of the game are strongly affected by the prevailing political ideology. The political mechanism, informal institutions, and especially the prevailing ideology all heavily influence the content of formal institutions, which in turn directly affects everyone's economic behavior and ultimately the nation's economic performance. Although the ideology of the citizens is an important factor forming the national ideology especially in a democratic society, the ideology of the political leaders is of paramount importance because it directly affects the form and direction of a nation's socio-economic institution. Which comes first: the ideology of the people or political leaders? This may be an important question but a difficult one to answer because both can and often do affect each other through the political feedback mechanism conducted by elections. However, the history of mankind reveals that in most of the successful development experiences, the ideology of political leader would carry more weight and constitutes the critical factor for economic development.

Ideology is the reflection of a vision of the world or the universe, the overall comprehension of things and events around us. The prevailing ideology governs ideals or objectives that a society, an individual, and political groups often value. While ideology is not necessarily based on logical reasoning but rather more often than not on normative judgment, it heavily influences one's view of the meaning of life, the concerns that political parties should pursue, and where society should be headed. Reflecting on the experiences of the past century, we can observe that ideology has exerted a dominant influence on economic policy making, and has to a great extent determined the content of economic institutions. It is in this sense that a country's economic institutions are influenced by ideology, and the people's behavior of a country is affected by the characteristics of its ideology. This is the reason why it is worth considering whether some aspects of the prevailing ideology are compatible with the fundamental nature of economic development. Needless to say, we may assume that a development-friendly ideology will contribute to economic development. Hence, as already implied above, the fundamental question for development is, "What is the nature of development-friendly institutions including ideology?" We will attempt an answer in the following sections.

History and Culture Can Be a Master but for Economic Progress Do Not Have to Be Slaves

Tradition and culture work just like ideology affecting the socio-economic behavior of members of a society and often are even stronger than the prevailing ideology in that they have become a generally accepted value for all the people. Therefore, they work as the general rules of the game that is widely accepted, whereas ideology is usually diversely shared among people. To some extent, tradition and culture work more or less on a similar level as religion. Path dependence, inertia, and network externalities in the process of institutional formation and its evolution are an important reason why tradition and culture have become so strong and persistent and are not easily changed. In this regard, it has been the case that economic success depends critically on whether the nature of a society's tradition and culture are development-friendly or not. In this sense, tradition as well as culture can be a master deciding the fate of society.

Having said this, however, exceptions do exist. There are examples of economies that have changed their development-unfriendly traditions and culture to become more development-friendly. For example, Park Chung Hee was able to change the Korean tradition and culture which powerfully affected the Korean way of thinking and behavior norms. For more than 500 years, as described by many observers, Koreans were viewed as lazy, sloppy, dependent, and inclined to blame heaven or others for their misfortunes and would prefer to pray to the heavens for help.[2] Korea's socio-economic policy regime under Park's leadership based on helping those who help themselves contradicted the existing

Korean tradition and culture, helping transform Koreans into people who helped themselves. A similar transformation can be found to have taken place in Singapore under their leader Lee Kwan Yew and also in China under Deng Xiao Ping. In this sense, for economic progress to occur, a society should not be a slave to development-unfriendly tradition and culture, and should make bold transformation towards becoming development-friendly.

History and culture are very stubborn and persistent institutions, which can only be transformed by the determined application of a different kind of institution. Whether this can be achieved is critically depending on the quality of leadership.

Essence of a New Theory of Economic Development

The essence of a new General Theory of Economic Development as developed in Jwa (2017) is summarized here.

A New Interpretation of the Function of Markets in the Capitalist Economy: Market as a Motivation Mechanism Based on Economic Discrimination (ED)

The role of markets in the context of development economics can be interpreted differently from the neoclassical "allocation economics" approach. The market in the real world, which is in fact much different from the perfectly competitive markets exhibited in textbooks, is an arena where economic agents exercise their discrimination power according to preferences, economic results and contributions. It thereby directs resources and wealth to successful agents, naturally and inevitably creating economic inequalities and motivating the agents to perform even better. Giving preferential treatment by directing greater economic resources and wealth to successful agents, the market motivates each participant to better help themselves and to work harder for their own success. Through this process, their micro-efforts are translated into the overall good of society in the form of economic development.

This economic discrimination and motivational function is in fact the essential role of the market that makes it an important institution for economic development. Here, "economic discrimination" is defined as treating differences differently and matching rewards with economic outcomes, thereby placing the right incentives for economic development.

It follows that the private property rights (PPR) system and economic freedom can be seen as an effective means for economic development because they allow for economic differences and inequalities, which motivate economic agents to improve themselves for their own economic betterment. In this regard, as history has demonstrated, the capitalist market economy with unfettered PPR and enhanced economic freedoms correlates strongly with economic growth and development. Simply put, any kind of institution that embodies economic discrimination can be viewed as development-friendly.

In the real world, we commonly find that consumers choose their preferred suppliers, banks as a lender tend to favor the better or more credit-worthy borrowers, investors invest their funds with the promising corporation, project, or entrepreneurs, companies hire the best workers, while workers on the other hand seek employment at the best or most promising companies, and assembly plants use the best quality parts suppliers, and so on and so forth. This list can go on endlessly. The point is precisely that a market consisting of all such economic agents collectively play a critical role as an economic discriminator in selecting, favoring and supporting the best (or better) economic performers by providing them with more purchasing power, more economic resources and more wealth, which in turn motivate every other participant to exert even greater effort to catch up with successful performers. This is the key role of the market as an important contributor to a country's economic change and development.

In essence, the market is the epitome of economic selection, differentiation and discrimination based on performances of market participants that helps motivate each economic agent to work harder and more effectively for their own economic progress. Consequently, the market encourages economic power concentration to accrue to the best market performers whether they be individuals, corporate organizations, and/or regions. This is an inevitable outcome in the pursuit of economic development.

General Features of Economic Development

Once the market's discrimination function is well understood, with a little thought it is easy to understand the following features of development: (1) increased economic concentration to better performers as a natural process of economic development; (2) increased economic power for better performing corporations; (3) rise of the middle-class and the wealthy class as a natural process of economic development; (4) emergence of big/mega cities and urban centers as a natural outcome of economic development. It should be noted here that the growth of better performing Small and Medium Sized Enterprises (SMEs) into larger, more powerful companies or simply the rise of bigger, competitive companies is a natural and inevitable process of economic development: economic development is a highly lopsided phenomenon.

The Nature of Development: Emergence of Complex Economy

Economic development should be understood as a type of emergent behavior of a complex economy transforming itself from a low-order into a higher-order economy: from the mail coach to the railroad, then to the automobile and the airplane-, and then to the spaceship economy. The system essentially becomes increasingly more complex through mutual exchanges of synergies created by non-linear interactions between economic actors. The process of synergy sharing takes place through the free-replication of (or free-riding on) others' success know-how by those interacting in the market place. This is in fact what is known as spill-over or the trickle-down process of external economic effects, which, however, implies the possibility of "market failure" in the developmental process. That is, and this is a subtle point, market often and do fail in fully rewarding successful performers who provide successful know-how to other economic agents, especially in the presence of potentially high (non-zero) transaction costs in the economy. That is, market failure works against creating sources of synergies or success know-how of star-performers and innovators in a systematic way. And as a result, market fails to exercise actively its economic discrimination function because it cannot effectively solve such free-riding problem on its own. The market left alone is hardly sufficient in creating economic development.

A little more elaboration may be useful. Market transactions involve the free and voluntary agreement on the terms of trade among trading partners. In contrast, an organization such as the corporation or the government will resort to authority or "command-and-control" for resource allocation, processing, and exchange within itself. What is important to note is that markets require a kind of negotiation process in reaching an agreement; i.e. some real negotiation costs are involved including search costs, shoe-leather cost, actual cash, and so on. Such costs collectively are known as transaction costs (or information costs) in the literature. Basically, market transactions can never be completely free from transaction costs. And as such, transaction costs that turn out to be prohibitively high can prevent market exchange from happening. Most importantly, markets involving exchange of synergy or successful know-how are characterized by very high transaction costs and are therefore prone to the kind of market failure referred to above; again, they often fail to fully reward those agents responsible for the synergy and/ or successful know-how. In short, free markets for positive synergies or know-how are plagued by this type of market failure.

Hence, markets left alone are not very good at producing the critical mass (of economically successful role models) needed to ignite economic transformation. This is what we refer here to as "market failure" of economic discrimination and motivation—a somewhat different interpretation of market failure and distinct from standard textbook definitions. Here, the introduction of a secure intellectual property right system may help improve the market's discrimination power but is usually not enough to solve the free-riding problem since synergy or know-how for success is intrinsically elusive to the extent that it is prohibitively costly to fully assign and enforce intellectual property right for it. It is such a way that the market economy is destined to be "trapped" in developmental failure, and this is in spite of the spread of the capitalist market economy and adoption of the private property right (PPR) system. Here, interestingly enough, the development process of the complex economy which involves learning from the success of others is destined to fail precisely because of the very nature of learning, which is characterized by free-riding on others' success knowhow.

The Critical Role of Corporate Organizations in Development

How does the firm or corporation help solve the kind of market failure problem we have discussed above? The private firm is an organization based on the command-control mechanism, which helps avoid (or save on) transaction costs (or information costs) as well as performs economic discrimination function for internal resource allocation.[3] A firm is thus an efficient economic discriminator alternative to the market in so far as the additional organizational costs incurred are less than the possible transaction costs of performing the same economic task via the market. Essentially, the firm solves market failure by internalizing knowhow free-riding activities and exercising the economic discrimination function efficiently. And as such, the corporate firm stimulates the creation of synergy or knowhow for success and helps expand the extent of the market by internalizing the high-transaction-costs-incurring synergy-creating-and-sharing process within it and expanding the list of new commodities (the order of complexity) in the market. According to this view, the corporate firm expands the actual imperfect market by cultivating a new market frontier which has not been utilized yet due to prohibitive transaction costs. In contrast, the theory of the firm popularized by Coase (1937) sees the firm as a substitute for a given perfect market at the margin with positive transaction costs; it, therefore, fails to see the market-expanding role of corporate firm in economic development.

Especially worth mentioning is the modern-day limited-liability corporation which is capable of performing such tasks economically at a much larger scale. The modern joint-stock corporation that developed spontaneously in the seventeenth century but had been legally banned over much of the eighteenth century and was finally legalized as a social technology in the early nineteenth century can be viewed as a kind of emergent complex system that evolved from the small individual and family-owned firms typical of the cottage industry era. Ever since its inception, the corporation has been an indispensable supplement to the market and a key locomotive for capitalist economic development. The corporation will seek and hire the best potential creators/sources of synergy or success knowhow, and actively discriminate and motivate them economically, thereby transforming the economy as well as the corporation itself to emerge into a higher-order system. It follows that the corporation is a key driver of economic development. Following Schumpeter, we view economic development as an emergent process of an economy that transforms itself into a railroad-economy jumping from the wagon-economy.[4] This process does not involve taking infinitesimal steps from a one-wagon to a ten-wagon economy. It is not just the addition of quantities, but an emergent process that is only possible via nonlinear interaction creating synergies when corporations work together with markets. The chances for markets alone of producing such transformative change are very slim.

Moreover, historically speaking, the modern corporation is perhaps a most distinctive feature of the modern capitalist economy; a revolution from the agrarian economy which also featured an active market system but did not spur economic development as we know it today. The modern development era is distinguished by humans living within corporate organizations which have substituted for land as a key means for survival, growth and development. In this way the modern capitalist corporate organizations have become the "home" for the middle income class by providing jobs to the peasants and liberating them from the Malthusian trap. In this regard, the private corporate organization becomes the source of middle income class as well as national wealth creation in the capitalist economy. Interestingly enough, the failed socialist experiments of the twentieth century all ended up with moving their economies back to an agrarian-type economy after their decades of history in nationalizing (or nullifying) the burgeoning modern private capitalistic corporations in their countries. From this perspective, one can argue that the modern capitalist economy can be appropriately called "a corporate economy" rather than simply referring to it as a "market economy".[5] One can argue further that its development will be a corporate-growth-led shared development by creating the middle income class.

The Indispensible Role of Government for Economic Development: Government-Led Economic Discrimination and Motivation

While the private corporation can reinforce economic discrimination under the umbrella of an "organization" without hindrance from transaction costs, it turns out that those successful corporations are also destined to become victims of free-riding as others imitate their success knowhow, and, therefore, the market economy again remains weak at producing a critical mass of successful corporations on a large-scale required for economic take-off and sustainable development. That is, while corporations help solve or, more precisely, avoid the kind of free-riding problem discussed above, it again faces the same free-riding problem through the actions of other corporations. In fact, this is exactly what we find, that most of the success knowhow of the successful corporations are usually exploited by catching-up and sometimes competing firms. Strengthening and reinforcing the intellectual property rights system may be of some help but is usually far from perfect. Therefore, it is a fact of life that, "successful corporations cannot be everlasting".

In this context, we now have a new rationale for the modern state as a "public" organization supplementing the functions of the market economy by way of promoting the growth and proliferation of corporations. Here, what is clearly discernible is the indispensable, positive role of the government as well as corporations for economic development. Governments should embody the same kind of economic discrimination mechanism as the market in order to alleviate the intrinsic failure of the market's economic discrimination function and by doing so act as the forerunner in a nation's economic development. The government is an institution that saves on transaction costs because by its very nature as an organization it is based on the command-and-control system. But there is an important trade off on savings on transaction costs by the government as it incurs organizational as well as additional inefficiency costs stemming from government bureaucracy.

But let us address more directly the question, "How should the government reinforce the market's economic discrimination function?" We have argued that the government should reinforce the market's discrimination function rather than intervene against what the market is doing, which is implied by traditional economic as well as political arguments. Pro-government industrial policy proponents, including those promoting egalitarian-type economic policies such as the social democratic and socialist camps have often argued for direct government intervention to correct and even reverse market outcomes. However, the new economic development theory proposed here suggests the opposite. As we have argued the market tends to fail in matching rewards with performances in the market in which synergy or knowhow for success exists for trade, thereby resulting in the failure of economic discrimination and failure in creating the incentives to grow on the part of corporations and individual agents necessary for economic development. The essential role of the government for economic development is, therefore, to alleviate such market failures by providing mechanisms to help those who help themselves so that they can contribute as important sources of synergy and successful knowhow.

In other words, unless the better performing corporations and individuals—the sources of success knowhow or synergy for economic emergence—are not fairly acknowledged and rewarded (discriminated) according to their respective contribution in the market due to transaction costs, the situation akin to Gresham's law will prevail and eventually drive them out of the market, leaving the whole society filled with mediocre economic performers. In the end, the chance for development by private market institutions and corporate organizations will become a remote possibility. It is here that the positive role of government becomes essential by supporting those better performing corporations and individuals who help themselves but are on the verge of being driven out of the market.

In this regard, the government should not intervene directly against market outcomes as some have suggested but rather should help re-enforce the market's discrimination function. Intervening against the market's discrimination function will discourage economic actors, resulting in sabotage and moral hazard, and ultimately work against economic development. Only by re-enforcing the market's discrimination function will the government encourage corporations and individuals to actively participate in the developmental process. This, we propose, is the important role of the government in national economic development.

It is important perhaps to stress that we are talking of economic discrimination and not political or social discrimination, the latter which we opposed for the obvious social and ethical reasons. But saying that we are in favor of political or social equality is not the same thing as being in favor of economic equality.

A new reinterpretation of successful industrial policy is therefore in order. From the new perspective of economic development process proposed in this book, industrial policy should be re-interpreted as an economic discrimination and motivational mechanism, as has been demonstrated by a number of economies during their catch-up period, including for example, Japan, Korea and China. In fact, the market can be interpreted as having exercised industrial policies "everyday" by picking the better performers and providing them with more resources according to their performance; that is, by exercising the economic discrimination function albeit imperfectly due to some unavoidable transaction costs. Note, as mentioned above, that the role of the government for economic development is to supplement and reinforce the market's economic discrimination function as well. That is, it should adopt a market-led industrial policy by helping those individuals and corporations who help themselves rather than working against or disregarding them in a non-discriminatory manner as implied by some mainstream neoclassical economists as well as egalitarian social democracy advocates. Industrial policy should pick market winners *ex post*, after the market outcome, rather than pick them *ex ante*, before the market outcome, which is precisely what markets do consistently.[6]

From this perspective, Japanese, Korean and Chinese industrial policies (IP) were successful precisely because they were implemented in an economically highly discriminatory manner so as to reinforce the market discrimination and motivation function. That is, these East Asian industrial policies tend to help those corporations that helped themselves, based on their market performances and in this sense perhaps should not be called "industrial policy" but rather discriminatory "corporate promotion policy" that corrects market and developmental failure.[7]

This feature of successful government policies, i.e. embodying economic discrimination, is not confined only to the case of successful industrial policy, but is also generally applicable to nearly any kind of economic policies. Broad observation reveals that successful economic policies turn out to be economically discriminatory while failed policies are largely egalitarian. As such, evidence is contrary to the popular egalitarian government intervention argument that the government should directly intervene and correct market outcomes and seek economic equalities in order to eliminate economic imbalances created by the market economy.

Political Ideology in Economic Development

The new theory supports an ideology that looks kindly at economic differences and inequalities as a natural process of economic development and thereby does not view the resulting outcomes of economic discrimination as a contradiction of the capitalist economy. And such an ideology should be viewed as development-friendly. The opposite kind of ideology, that is, one antagonistic to economic differences and inequalities and favoring economic equalities including equal economic outcomes should be viewed as development-unfriendly.

It is often touted that the two wheels of the democratic cart are liberty and equality. The issue with liberty is that it seems easily subdued by the egalitarian ethos, especially when it comes to modern-day democracies that emphasize "equal rights." Central to an ideal democracy, for example, is the "one man one vote" system, which easily lends itself to egalitarian ethos. This egalitarianism tends to permeate into all aspects of not only political but also economic life, being translated into "equal opportunity" in economic capability or "equal outcome", while diminishing or sometimes even neglecting "equality before the law". This adversely affects economic development, because as we have mentioned, economic development is based on economic discrimination, which egalitarianism is diametrically opposed to. Note that only "equality before the law" is consistent with the market's economic discrimination function. "Equality of outcomes" implies a socialist economy while "equal opportunity" is not much different from "equal outcome" if interpreted

Table 4.1 Political-economy matrix of social order

Political order	(A) Liberty (equal political rights)	(B) Authoritarian
Economic order	(C) Economic Discrimination (ED)	(D) Egalitarianism (equal outcome)

Source Jwa and Yoon (2004a)

as equality in economic capabilities. Note that "opportunity" as well as "outcome" is an economically valuable good which can only be obtained in a costly way by hard working agents and is difficult to be equally and freely provided by the government or anybody else.

Table 4.1 above represents the spectrum of political and economic order. The top row represents political order ranging from liberty (A) to authoritarian (B), and the bottom row represents the economic order ranging from economic discrimination (C) to egalitarianism (D). Accordingly, we can classify a political economy regime into four different combinations of political order and economic order. That is, A + C for "market democracy", A + D for "social democracy", B + C for "developmental state", and B + D for "totalitarian regime". Here, it can easily be seen that A + C and B + C are development-friendly because they adopt economic discrimination policies while A + D and B + D are development-unfriendly because they dismiss economic discrimination and follow egalitarianism. Seen from this perspective, as far as economic development is concerned, the political order—whether democratic or authoritarian—is not as critical as the choice of the economic order. Even politically authoritarian states can be development-friendly if they adopt economically discriminatory or economic discrimination policies. On the other hand, even liberal democracies can lead to economic stagnation if they champion economic egalitarianism; a typical example is social democracy that adopts an economically egalitarian regime.

Finally note that the four-regime classification presented above can be contrasted with the two-regime classification, inclusive versus extractive institutions, proposed by Acemoglu and Robinson (2012). Although in the two-dimensional classification, placing the totalitarian state as an extractive institutions and the egalitarian democracy as an inclusive institution is pretty straight forward, this classification fails to consider further the properties of the developmental state and market democracy. In the context of the two-regime classification, it is not clear whether the developmental state can be inclusive or exclusive. More importantly, contrary to Acemoglu and Robinson, the egalitarian democracy regime, although an inclusive institution, is not developmental friendly when viewed under the economic discrimination perspective with our four-regime classification.

Creation of Development-Friendly Ideology

A critical question then is, "How do we create a development-friendly ideology and state?" The examples of sustainable growth and development imply that repeated application of economic institutions and policies based on the economic discrimination principle have helped change peoples' ideology toward becoming more development-friendly. The first condition for this change is a political leadership that understands and endorses the economic discrimination principle and is determined to lead the nation's political ideology that is consistent with the economic discrimination principle. The second condition is a kind of firewall that must be built between economic policy-making and politics, especially one that insulates economic policy from egalitarian populism. Examples of such economic discrimination leadership that had succeeded in changing the nation's ideology towards becoming development-friendly include that of Meiji Japan, Park Chung Hee in Korea, Lee Kwan Yew in Singapore, Deng Xiao Ping in China, Margaret Thatcher in England, Manmohan Singh in India, Mahathir Mohamad in Malaysia and to some degree Ronald Reagan in the US. In contrast, it is very difficult to find cases of economic take-off and sustainable development without leadership that embodied development-friendly or economic discrimination ideology.

Can-Do Spirit or Self-Help Spirit as the Key Development-Friendly Ideology

An exemplary development-friendly ideology is the "can-do spirit" or "self-help spirit" which is usually instilled as a peoples' way of thinking only by the continuous enforcement of an economically discriminatory policy regime, on top of ideological education and/or propaganda. Similarly, tradition and culture as an institution can also be transformed into a development-friendly institution by the repeated application of economically discriminatory institutions and policies. For example, historically, Korean people were said to be lazy, dependent and hardly motivated for economic progress; in other words, development-unfriendly. However, Korea's "can-do spirit" or "self-help spirit" observed during its modernization era, which was surprising given Korea's historical and cultural tradition, turns out to have been created by the repeated application of the government's discriminatory economic policies that helped only those who helped themselves. This includes the Saemaul Undong (or New Village) movement, export-promotion policies, and industrial policy promoting heavy and chemical industry, all to be discussed later.

Consolidation and Implications of the New Theoretical Framework

Consolidation of the Arguments

The economic discriminatory institutions, formal as well as informal, embodying the principle of treating economic differences differently, i.e. the economic discrimination paradigm, and respecting the ideology of helping those who help themselves, are essential for development. However, egalitarian institutions that ignore or try to reverse economic differences tend to disregard economic excellence and therefore hinder economic prosperity. Markets cum private property rights system plus economic freedom may be excellent ingredients for the survival or moderate growth of an economy, but they need to be supplemented by economic discrimination policies of the government and private organizations if there is to be any real chance for economic take-off and economic development. Seen from this perspective, economic discrimination is a necessary condition for economic development, while economic egalitarianism is a sufficient condition for economic stagnation.[8]

In fact, economic discrimination and motivation by the market, as well as the government and corporation, are necessary conditions for economic development. This is the key message of the condensed development experiences of Japan, Korea and China, as well as the extended Western development experiences as will be further discussed in the next chapter.[9]

The General Theory of Economic Development is succinctly summarized in Fig. 4.2, which depicts the spaces of the three institutions of economic development consisting of the market, corporations and the government. The circles represent the economic space that each institution occupies. Each of these institutions on their own could do little to spur a nation's economic development. For instance, markets embody economic discrimination, as economic winners are selected constantly,

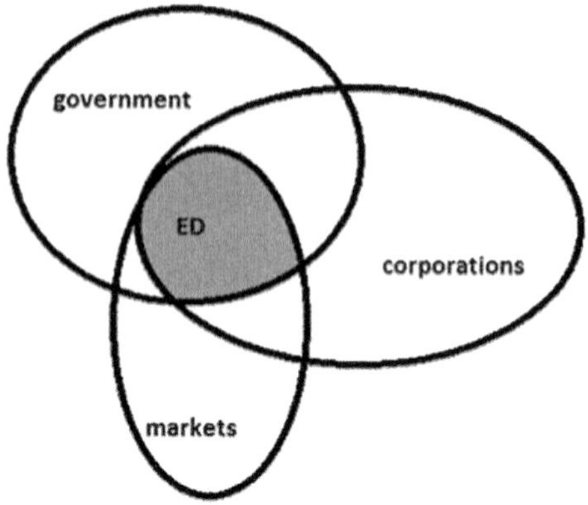

Fig. 4.2 Economic development and economic discrimination (ED). *Souce* Jwa (2017)

but on their own, market failure greatly reduces the capacity of economic development. Only by the economic joining of the three institutions (i.e. 'the holy trinity') can economic discrimination be magnified and the great engine of economic development ignited. Thus we have here a clear answer as to what kinds of institutions (organizations as well as 'rules of the game') matter for economic growth and development—institutions that embody the economic discrimination principle! For economic development, the government, corporations and markets must concur with the economic discrimination principle, each respecting the other to elevate successful entities and behavior and thereby deliver economic development. Figure 4.2 highlights the central area where the three institutions of development—the government, markets and corporations—overlap and are conjoined by the economic discrimination (ED) principle which allows its magnification and translation into economic growth and development.

It is perhaps worth stressing that economic discrimination is the mechanism that creates competition and wealth and is certainly not about protecting insiders. It is a mechanism that is meant to motivate economic agents, including the government and corporations as well as individuals, to seek success which helps extend markets by reinvigorating dormant economies. It is true that with economic discrimination come all kinds of imbalances as well as inequality in resources and wealth. It does not guarantee an ideal scenario by any means, but at least it guarantees wealth and prosperity to some degree. The concentration of economic power by successful players is inevitable, because economic development is an uneven process. However, any attempts at diminishing economic differences by mitigating economic discrimination through policy often leads to economic stagnation as incentives become distorted. This is a serious mistake as it removes the very engine of economic growth and development. We may even mention here that by mitigating economic discrimination, egalitarianism becomes a sufficient condition for economic stagnation. Be that as it may, we strongly warn that egalitarianism negates and could even reverse economic progress.

Important Implications on the Role of Government and Market

The debate between government-led vs. market-led development have thus far been misguided. An alternative view is that governments and markets both are necessary parts of the economic development puzzle, according to the new perspective of economic development. Economics should go beyond the simplistic view of government versus market and rather adopt a holistic view of the economy in which both entities are needed for economic development.

According to mainstream argument, the role of government is assumed to be an essential supplier of physical as well as institutional SOC including education, R&D, private property right system, and the rule of law. However, according to the new perspective, the key developmental role of government beyond its traditional role is to reform the informal as well as formal institutions (i.e. rules of the game, especially institutional constraints) into one that incorporates the spirit of helping those who help themselves, i.e. the spirit of market's discrimination function. Such motivational institutions are favorable for economic development. Occasionally, it is necessary to resort to moral suasion to educate people to believe in and act along with the ideology of "God helps those who help themselves". In this regard, national leadership should follow the principle of economic discrimination and encourage people to believe in self-help and hard work. Seen from this perspective, the government as a whole should avoid intervening against market outcomes and avoid egalitarian policies which will nullify the market's discrimination function and private sector's incentives to grow.

In conclusion, the market, corporations, and the government should all exercise economic discrimination for the sake of economic development. This all-out economic discriminatory effort motivates people to seek self-help which will instill the "can-do" spirit as the leading developmental ideology of the society. Development is not a type of public good that can be easily achievable simply by adding capital, labor, and technology as the neoclassical growth theory would argue. Rather, development is a rare phenomenon which takes place only if economic discrimination by all three players (market, corporation and government) is simultaneously exercised.[10] In this regard, we claim that the market, corporations and the government form the "holy trinity of economic development." And as we have said, economic discrimination is a necessary condition for economic development.

So when then does developmental failure occur? Given that economic egalitarianism is a sufficient condition for economic stagnation, egalitarian economic institutions working against the market's economic discrimination function will discourage people from economizing and seeking economic development, which leads to economic stagnation. Government's supportive policies that run against the economic discrimination principle of helping those who help themselves will eventually fail to contribute to economic progress. In particular, egalitarian policy with a "one-over-n" (1/n) supportive system cannot generate developmental dynamism into an economy.

Implications on Macroeconomic Growth and Productivity Analysis

The new General Theory of Economic Development implies that the growth and development of the "capitalist" or "corporate" economy is in fact the process of corporate-growth-led shared growth in that corporate growth causes the rise of the middle income class as well as national wealth. This further suggests a very important alternative perspective to the existing model of macroeconomic growth and productivity analysis based on the neoclassical production function concept.

A simplified version of the mainstream market-centric model assumes that a nation's aggregate output (Y) is a function of aggregate capital (K), labor (L), and technology (T), or $Y = f(K, L, T)$. Note that such typical market models are void of the corporate firm by having only a production function instead. This neoclassical production function implies that the market will in a somewhat mystical way produce output Y, given resources (K, L, and T) which are provided by the economy or the society. In this regard, this model may properly be called a "market" production function because the market is the grand aggregator of the factors of production. While this model has its uses for some simplified analytical purposes, it also has a number of problems.

First, the neo-classical formulation does not treat holistically the nature of economic change; i.e., it does not treat the emergent behavior of corporate firms because the firm is reduced to its constituent parts, K, L, and T based on a purely reductionist perspective. The production function model seems to imply that even without the corporate firm (just as in the socialist economy), economic growth and development may arise as far as money, people, and scientists are accounted for. It is interesting to observe that the economics profession and management scientists maintain the argument that the eighteenth and nineteenth centuries' Industrial Revolution was led by advances in science and technology and the resulting productivity increase without mentioning the institutional innovation of corporate firms. However, it is important to note that technology (or even any other production factors for this matter) by itself cannot be translated into economic development unless there exists a corporate firm which can transform technology, and its externalities, into the useful economic commodities.[11] Once anyone becomes trapped into the traditional production function perspective, it is easy to believe, for example, that the old Soviet economy having only factories but no corporations could catch up with the US economy in a foreseeable future thanks to the speed of the former's scientific development and the resulting growth performance in her earlier years as one renowned economist expected.[12] Second, even leaving aside this issue, the production function approach has serious problems with the measurement of factors of production, K, L and T which cannot be measured with any reasonable precision, reducing the empirical usefulness of the approach.

My new General Theory as explained presents an alternative approach to macroeconomic growth and productivity analysis. Jwa (2017) propose a "corporate" production function which sees the corporate firms as the grand aggregator of national productive resources, K, L and T, in the private sector and adopts the total corporate assets in the economy as the aggregate factors of production. This corporate production function can be expressed as $Y = f(CA)$ where Y is per capita income, and CA is the per capita corporate asset defined as total sum of individual firms' asset in their respective balance sheet divided by the population in national economy. The reason why this approach uses per-capita measurement by factoring out the labor input (L) is because the corporate asset in corporate accounts does not include the value of human resources specifically.[13]

In addition, a shared growth hypothesis can also be tested by estimating the equation specifying income distribution (measured by the Gini coefficient) as a function of CA, Gini = g(CA).

This alternative approach has a number of advantages over the traditional market production function. First, it does not require any cumbersome measurement problem of capital and technology which are already consolidated into the CA by the corporate sector. Second, it can help easily identify the nation's aggregate productivity of corporate sector because CA can be interpreted as consolidating individual factors except for labor input and therefore, as taking into account even the synergy or cross partial effects among them. Moreover, it provides us a holistic picture of macroeconomic growth and productivity of the economy. Third, the residuals from this alternative specification of production can be utilized for further analysis on the impacts of tangible as well as intangible social infrastructures including social institutions provided by the public sector. Note that CA does not include such social infrastructures, so the impact can be analyzed by the residual estimates, not unlike the traditional TFP analysis for the market production function approach. In this case, if the physical SOC capital is estimated and added up to the CA, then the residual terms can be interpreted as reflecting the efficiency of intangible social institutions like economic institutions. This helps improve the empirical analysis on the impacts of economic institutions on growth according to the new institutional approach. However, data availability of CA for the whole corporate sector and also its accuracy is limited because typical balance sheet data of SM&E in particular and the self-employed firms in general are usually not available; also they may not be fully compatible with international standards. On this account, the improvement of the data on CA is a necessary precondition for improving the usefulness of the corporate production function approach.

The corporate production function model will be utilized in empirically evaluating the rise and fall of Korean economic performances from the perspective of corporate-growth-led shared growth in Chap. 7.

Notes

1. This is one of the main argument of the New Institutional Economics (NIE) perspective of North (1990) and others.
2. See for example Bishop (1970) who writes that such development-unfriendly behavior was characteristic of the late nineteenth century

Korea, which had been due to the long history of extractive institutions of the Chosun dynasty. She also found that Korean migrants in Eastern Russia at that time turned out to be relatively industrious and become prosperous under the protection of private property rights.

3. See Jwa (2017) for more details of the twin functions of the firm; i.e. transaction costs saver as well as economic discriminator.
4. See note 1, p. 64, Schumpeter (1974).
5. This point can be interpreted as a variation of Simon's argument that an economic system is better called the organizational economy rather than the market economy. See Simon (1991).
6. There is temptation to determine the winners ex-ante but this will usually fail because of information imperfection and often may not be distinguishable from chance. Here the point is not to say that governments and market disregard the possibility of determining the winners ex-ante entirely, but rather if they do so they will not be successful, and will have no choice but to base their decisions on ex-post results and observations.
7. More detailed manual for successful corporate promotional policy will be provided in Chap. 7.
8. Jwa and Yoon (2004a, b).
9. See Jwa (2017) for further elaboration.
10. See Jwa (2017).
11. Even Peter Drucker (1993) who rightly recognized the emergence of the joint-stock company during the Industrial Revolution failed to recognize its importance relative to technological progress as one of the key factors for the Industrial Revolution.
12. Paul Samuelson (1989, p. 837) stated 2 years before the collapse of the Soviet Union, "Contrary to what many skeptics had earlier believed, the Soviet economy is proof that... a socialist command economy can function and even thrive." after a continuous update of the projection of the Soviet Union catching up with the US which started from the 1967 edition of his Economics.
13. Here, if the corporate production function is assumed as a linear form as $Y = a + bCA + \varepsilon$, then Y can be interpreted as permanent annuity flow, the coefficient of CA, "b" as discount rate and CA as the sum of the present values of discounted annuity flows Y discounted by "b". In other words, the stock of national productive assets, CA creates the income flows Y at the rate of "b", the nation's marginal productivity. The constant term, "a" can be interpreted as per capita income of the purely agrarian economy void of any corporate production. Here, using the per capita concept for income, Y as well as corporate asset, CA by factoring out labor input is same as assuming the function, $Y = f(CA)$ is linear homogenous. See Jwa (2017) for more details on this model.

References

Acemoglu, Daron, and James A. Robinson. 2012. *Why Nations Fail: The Origins of Power, Prosperity, and Poverty*. New York: Crown Publishers.

Bishop, Isabella Bird. 1970 [1897]. *Korea and Her Neighbors*. Seoul: Yeonsei University Press.

Coase, Ronald H. 1937. The Nature of the Firm. *Economica* 4 (16): 386–405.

Drucker, Peter. 1993. *Post-Capitalist Society*. New York: Harper Business, A Division of HarperCollins Publishers.

Jwa, Sung-Hee. 2017. *A General Theory of Economic Development: Towards A Capitalist Manifesto*. Cheltenham: Edward Elgar.

Jwa, Sung-Hee, and Yong Yoon. 2004a. Political Institutions and Economic Development: A Study in Economic Discrimination and Political Philosophy. *Seoul Journal of Economics* 17 (3): 275–307.

Jwa, Sung-Hee, and Yong Yoon. 2004b. A New Look at Development Economics through Korea's Experience: The Paradox of Economic Development. Paper Presented at the 2004 KDI-KAEA Conference, Seoul.

North, Douglass. 1990. *Institutions, Institutional Change and Economic Performance*. Cambridge: Cambridge University Press.

Samuelson, Paul. 1989. *Economics*, 13th ed. New York: McGraw Hill.

Schumpeter, Joseph A. 1974 [1934]. *The Theory of Economic Development, translated by Redvers Opie*. Oxford: Oxford University Press.

Simon, Herbert A. 1991. Organization and Market. *Journal of Economic Perspectives* 5 (2): 25–44.

CHAPTER 5

An Overview of Global Economic Development Experiences

Abstract This chapter reviews the global development experiences from the Industrial Revolution to the modern era under the lenses of the new General Theory of Economic Development. The chapter begins by explaining the differences in economic development between the pre- and post-Industrial Revolution periods. The author emphasizes the role of demographic change and the establishment of corporations as well as the importance of economic discrimination policies for economic take-off. This is contrasted to the problems of social democracy and egalitarianism in the post WWII era of economic slowdown and decline. A political-economy axis of social order is adopted to summarize development trends in various countries.

Keywords Pre- and post-industrial revolution · Joint-stock company Agrarian vs. capitalist economy · Corporate economy · Egalitarianism Social democracy · Egalitarian democracy

S.-H. Jwa, *The Rise and Fall of Korea's Economic Development*,
DOI 10.1007/978-3-319-58065-4_5

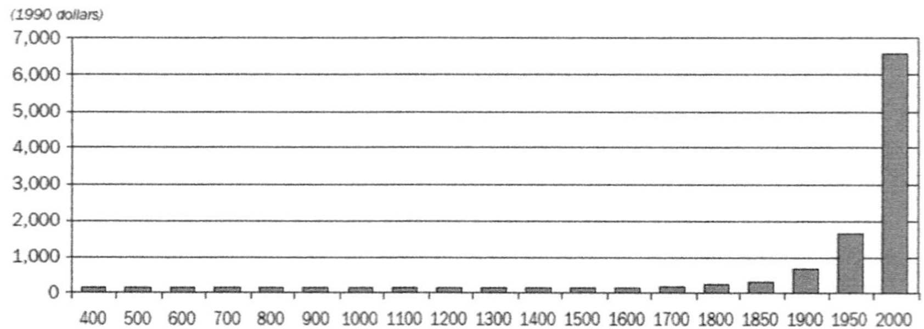

Fig. 5.1 Average world GDP per capita, 400–2000. *Source* http://econ161.berkeley.edu/tceh/1998_draft/world_gdp/estimating_world_gdp.html

Explaining the Difference in Economic Development Between Pre- And Post-industrial Revolution Era

Economic development as we know it today began only since the 19th century following the British Industrial Revolution (see Fig. 5.1). For long period of time up until the 18th century, human societies were plagued by very poor economic conditions, so-called Malthusian trap. The point is that economic transformation is rare and is only a recent phenomenon. So, "What factors made such unprecedented economic transformation possible?"

Changes in Demographic Structure and Economic Institutions

Firstly, the education and growth of the middle-class was an important demographic change. Before the Industrial Revolution, Britain's fertility rate had been stagnant with only the upper middle class having higher fertility rates. Hence the educated middleclass with their growing population increasingly mixed with and eventually substituted the uneducated lower class, resulting in the spread of educated people across Britain.[1] Knowledge of successful knowhow rapidly propagated to the whole population, becoming common among the general public.

Secondly, economic freedom including human rights became the basis for individuals' economic creativity and ingenuity. Great Britain was a pioneer in limiting the powers of the monarch and paving the road for championing the individual as well as their economic rights, thereby laying the foundation for the Industrial Revolution.

Thirdly, the protection of private property rights (PPR) became the basis for the development and proliferation of the market economy firing the economic imagination of the general public. Britain introduced the private property rights system early on with the Glorious Revolution and made enormous strides in the improvement of individual economic freedoms.[2]

Legalization of Limited-Liability, Joint-Stock Company System

The joint-stock company is undoubtedly a higher-order complex organizational form of the firm beyond the traditionally family- or individually-owned firm. Under the joint-stock company, large amounts of capital can be made available from the enlarged base of stock holders thanks to the system of limited-liability stock allowing for high-risk business ventures. The joint-stock company system that first formed spontaneously in the 17th century was banned in the 18th century by the Bubble Act in 1720 requiring the parliamentary charter. In the early 19th century, it was again allowed to blossom with the repeal of the Bubble Act in 1825 and first became institutionalized in Britain under the Joint-Stock Companies Act of 1844. Since the early 19th century, even before the formal introduction of the system, similar forms of companies appeared that helped commercialize various technological innovations and discoveries.

And as already mentioned, the joint-stock company is perhaps the most innovative social technology ever discovered by humankind since the agricultural revolution. It has since played an instrumental role allowing nonlinear interaction in the economy. The joint-stock company was indeed the key driver of the British Industrial Revolution.

Role of Government as an Economic Discriminator and Economic Motivator

What is important to realize is that the British government at the time played an important role as promoter of economic development by providing various social technologies such as individual economic freedom, private property rights system, the joint-stock company system, and the general education system. In fact, the system helped re-enforce the market discrimination function, thereby helping create the spirit of self-help and encouraged economic agents to pursue economic progress and wealth, regardless of whether the government understood the economic discrimination role or not and whether it intended the positive outcome. Before the Revolution, however, the economic discrimination (ED) role of government was not well understood and the government was in fact extractive and destructive to economic development by not allowing the growth of such institutions that helped promote the market's economic discrimination function.

Emergence of the Corporate Economy From the Agrarian Economy by the Power of Corporation

In the pre-industrial Revolution era, the agrarian, wagon-type economy based on agriculture was under immense pressure suffering from the Malthusian trap. However, in the post-industrial revolution era, the railroad-, automobile-, airplane-, or spaceship-economy, i.e., the corporatized-industrial capitalist economy, firmly based on the corporation became the driving force of the modern economy. Success and failure of corporations become a key factor in determining the rise and fall of national economies; the corporation was the engine of economic development for the industrialized capitalist economy. In this sense, the capitalist economy can be labeled a corporate economy rather than a market or simply industrial economy.

It is interesting to note that most of the enlightened commentators on the British Industrial Revolution emphasized the importance of technological innovation as the prime cause of the Revolution. They failed to recognize the key role of the joint-stock capitalist corporations: the sense that technological innovation would be of no use for economic development unless important social technology like corporate firms could transform the technological ideas into useful commodities in mass.[3]

Economic Changes in Post-industrial Revolution Era

Western Capitalist Economies in 20th Century Before and During the Cold War Era

Following the Industrial Revolution in Britain, other European countries such as Germany, France, and the US immediately replicated the British successful knowhow to catch-up with Britain, thereby opening up the Western era of global economic leadership in 20th century. Industrial policy was indeed the strategy adopted by late-comers to catch up with Great Britain. The US gradually overtook the British economic hegemony from the late-19th century to the turn of the century by capitalizing on the modern joint-stock company system which was the creation of Britain but burgeoned in the US, leading her own Industrial Revolution. Germany was active in this regard, led by industrial policies advocated by Friedrich List. Later, Japan replicated Germany as well as Britain and eventually joined the Western nations in terms of economic development. Japan turned out to have the most successful industrial policy and was a successful imitator of Western developmental knowhow.

Perhaps the most significant success factor of Western economies is that they accepted the inevitability of unequal economic outcomes created by economic discrimination in the capitalist market economy. Economic discrimination by the market, corporations as well as the government was accepted as a fact of life. Democratic egalitarian ethos had not yet featured heavily into economic life, at least not before the communist revolution and the notorious Cold War. Roughly speaking, up until the mid-20th century, the capitalist economies had enjoyed strong economic expansion thanks to unfettered economic discrimination mechanism of the market and governments, and the growth of corporations throughout the Western hemisphere.

During the Cold War era, however, the capitalist economies increasingly adopted a revised capitalism, a welfare state or social democratic regime to cope with the egalitarian appeal of the socialist bloc by introducing egalitarian economic policies into the capitalist market economy. The government's role suddenly sought equal income and development, through redistribution and welfare policies accompanied by high taxes. Such a policy stance became popular with developed as well as newly independent developing economies. Towards the end of the 20th century, many capitalist market economies became so-called "mixed economies" but with more or less socialist ideology, and many adopted social democracy principles. Since then the socialist bloc eventually collapsed due to their obvious economic development contradictions, except for North Korea, which is on the binge of collapse clinging on desperately for survival.

Social Democracy (SD): A Panacea for The 21st Century?

General Argument

Socialist economies have failed miserably in fulfilling the high expectation of an egalitarian society. The unfettered egalitarianism that permeated into the economic realm of a society turned out to be a disappointment because it had worked against the economic discrimination mechanism of economic life as we have stressed with the new economic development paradigm. In this regard, we find many instances of capitalist economies facing serious dilemma having already succumbed to socialist ideology in the name of social democracy (or "revised capitalism") within their own systems even as the socialist economies have faded away. Social democracy has aimed at minimizing economic inequality which is intrinsically built into the economic discrimination mechanism of true capitalist economic systems. The same applies to revised capitalism. Therefore, it seems to be the case that the capitalist economies under social democracy

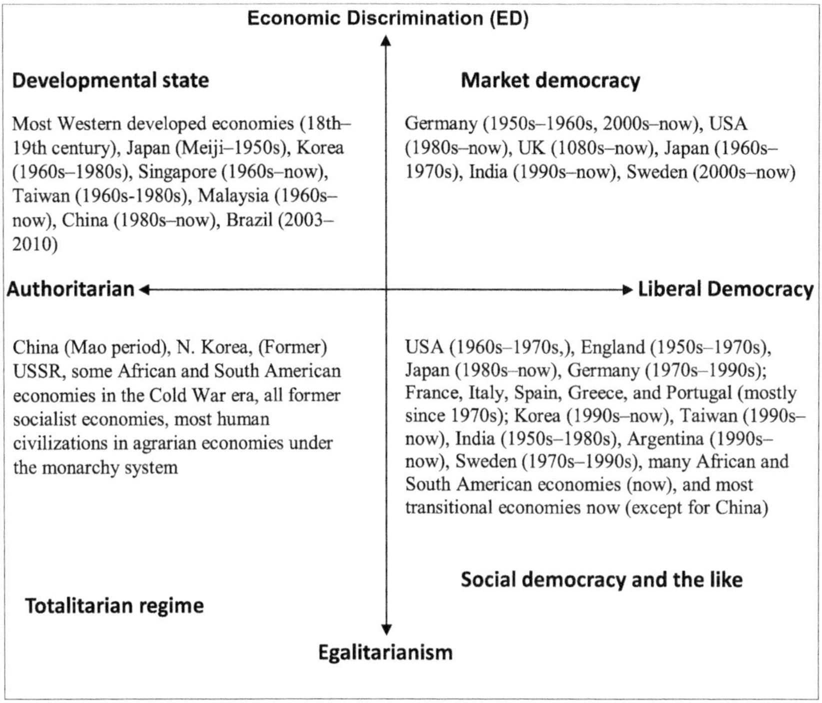

Fig. 5.2 Political-economy axis of social order and application. *Source* Jwa (2017)

possess within itself serious contradictory elements with egalitarianism working against its own progress. Most economies adopting social democracy have been disappointing regardless of whether they are developed or underdeveloped nations; all have deteriorated economically during the past several decades or so.

Furthermore, even the formally-labeled liberal market democratic system has not performed well, and there seems no sign of change largely because of the modern-day "one-man-one-vote" democracy which inevitably pushed the regime towards populism. Populism has a tendency to extend the egalitarian ethos beyond the political realm, often contaminating economic life. Regardless of formalism, these democracies seem unable to avoid the egalitarian trap, turning into a de facto social democracy where the economic discrimination mechanism has been largely sacrificed. The now widely adopted social democratic system poses a huge risk of becoming a dangerous poison for the late-coming developing countries, and also for developed countries as well.

Actual Development Experiences

General Observation

Adopting the framework of the political-economy axis of social order based on the new perspective of development theory presented in Table 4.1 in the previous chapter, it is not difficult to consistently classify the diverse experiences of economies as shown in Fig. 5.2. It is interesting to note that many economies now fall into the category of development-unfriendly, egalitarian democracies except for a few. Many economies have moved away from the totalitarian regime represented in the 3rd quadrant, such as the old monarchy system or the 20th century socialist economies, to the developmental state (4th quadrant) and to market democracy (1st quadrant) where they have tried to stay, but somehow have failed as they adopted some kind of social democratic regimes (2nd quadrant). Most seem to have fallen into the economic egalitarian trap, thereby becoming development-unfriendly.

Experiences of Social democratic, developed countries

In general, what seems to have happened is that most of the failed socialist countries have adopted a social democracy seeking development-unfriendly egalitarian economic policy. In the same vein, other countries include the now struggling European social democracies, the populist democracies of South America including Argentina, and some Sub-Saharan African economies that gained independence and adopted democratization in the post-war period. Over the sustained period in the post-war era they exhibited continuously declining (and some negative) long-term growth trend and now suffer from various economic difficulties including poor growth performance, worsening income distribution and precarious financial soundness of the government.

As for the relatively developed economies under social democracy that also appear under the guise of revised capitalism and welfare state, all have or had experienced sluggish economic performances in the last several decades. England under the welfare state in the post war era suffered from serious economic woes until the Thatcher reform in the 1980s. Germany also experienced declining growth since the 1970s under its social democratic policy regime (so-called German disease) until the Schröder reform in 2003 under the Agenda 2010. Germany as well as England did away with their egalitarian economic policies in favor of development-friendly ED-based market democracies, thereby experiencing relatively better economic performances. France remains under a social democratic egalitarian trap and economic performance has continued to be poor since the WWII. Other nations like Japan which has also adopted a social democratic policy regime since the late 1970s and the Portugal, Italy, Greece and Spain (PIGS) economies, which have been under social democracy for long, have not yet reformed their egalitarian policy regime and as a consequence continue to suffer from economic stagnation.

Sweden is an interesting case, being a relatively exceptional country; it demonstrates how a strong-corporate-sector based social democracy can be relatively safe from the usual economic weaknesses of social democracy. Sweden had sought a Schumpeterian path towards a socialist economy since the early 20th century, and not by a communist revolution, but by the nationalization of large corporations through a democratic political process.[4] Even so, for that purpose, Sweden all along continued to promote its strong corporate base that would eventually become nationalized. However, since the globalization era, Sweden experienced increasingly weakening international competitiveness and an economic crisis in the early 1990s. Facing economic difficulties at the time, Sweden fortunately gave up its long-time vision to adopt a socialist economy in midst of the widespread collapse of the socialist bloc and it has successfully reformed its extremely egalitarian policies and has rebounded with relatively good growth. The economy's main strength lies in its relatively strong corporate sector, which has supported Sweden's heavy dependence on its redistributive welfare system.

On the other hand, it turns out that the US followed a different path from the European social democratic developed economies by being somewhat passive in adopting social democracy beyond so-called revised capitalism. But recently the policy landscape has been tilting toward a more egalitarian policy regime under Obama's leadership. The 2008 subprime mortgage financial crisis has not helped, as much of the finger pointing has been directed to the rich for various economic ills including the nation's income inequalities.

Experiences of newly industrialized/industrializing economies

Some developing economies which have exhibited economic dynamism for a sustained period all turn out to have adopted economic discrimination embedded in their economic policies. For example, Singapore and Hong Kong have for quite some time adopted the economic discrimination paradigm. They attracted the world's best companies by setting up various incentives which in turn have helped their economies to grow rapidly. For example, Singapore uses specific programs that favor better manpower not only economically but also even in social life. In a similar vein, Dubai can be highlighted as an important city that has attracted the world's best people and corporations through special incentives.

China is perhaps the most conspicuous and recent example of the power of economic discrimination economic policies. In recent history, when Deng Xiao Ping became China's Premiere in the late-1970s and implemented the ideology of "the rich-led nation" in various institutional settings, he had effectively amplified the economic discrimination function of the market. China thus encouraged its citizen's zeal for becoming rich and the transformation has allowed the nation to experience remarkable growth for more than 30 years, even under a nondemocratic and relatively less free socialist market-economic system.

India turned towards establishing a capitalist market system in the mid-1980s after difficult economic situations under a social democratic regime inherited with its independence from Britain. India can now look forward to an era of sustained growth.

Lessons from the global economic developmental experiences

From the somewhat brief overview of global development experiences, some important lessons for take-off and sustainable development are as follows.

First, the economic discrimination mechanism of the capitalist economy should not be sacrificed. If at all, economic discrimination should be promoted if there is to be economic take-off and development.

Second, business corporations should be afforded economic freedoms, and proper incentives should be in place to allow them to act as the primary engine for economic growth and development in the capitalist society.

Third, the government should exercise economic discrimination to support business corporations as well as individuals by creating and building appropriate institutions. Egalitarianism in economic policy should be mitigated as this will demoralize and de-motivate economic agents, i.e., acts as a dangerous disincentive for growth that will hurt economic dynamism.

Fourth, social democracies all have faced and continue to face serious economic difficulties because the economically egalitarian policy regimes have destroyed incentives for growth. From the economics perspective, social democracy is not much different from socialism or even communism. This is especially true in relation to the economic incentive structure or economic order because these regimes are in fact seeking the same economic order of equality as socialism despite differences in major aspects of their political order. We warn, however, that social democracy is destined to economic failure because it works against the economic discrimination principle in the same way as the failed socialist economies.

Fifth, 20th century global economic development experiences testify clearly to the fact that economic discrimination correlates with economic development while economic egalitarianism does not. Successful, dynamically emerging economies (e.g. China, Singapore, Korea, India, Hong Kong, Dubai, Taiwan and others, at some stage in their recent histories) all have or had embraced the economic discrimination paradigm, paving the road for those who help themselves. Adopting the ideology of "God help those who help themselves", taking on business-friendly, FDI friendly,[5] and corporate-friendly policies and free-riding on early movers, they have provided the right incentives for economic agents. And by encouraging competition through government-led economic discrimination to augment market rivalry, these economies have achieved high economic growth and development. Simply put, the right incentives for growth were created by placing economic discrimination in the policy regime. On the other hand, most economies that adopted a social democratic system by implementing egalitarian economic policies such as a strong redistribution policy cum high tax rate have all experienced a continuously stagnating economy.

Sixth, the key lessons of 20th century economic development can be succinctly summarized as follows: "Economic discrimination is a necessary condition for economic development while economic egalitarianism is a sufficient condition for economic stagnation".

Notes

1. See Clark (2007).
2. See North (1990), North and Thomas (1973) and North and Weingast (1989) for the related arguments.
3. Peter Drucker (1993) may be an exception in rightly recognizing the emergence of joint-stock company during the industrial revolution but he strongly advocates the technological innovation as the key factor for the

revolution while fails to recognize the importance of the joint-stock company.

4. See Schumpeter (1942) for his argument supporting socialism. For more on Swedish vision for Schumpeterian socialist's path, see Henrekson, Magnus and Ulf, Jakobsson (2001).
5. Reliance on FDI turned out to be different depending on the countries' need as well as attractiveness for FDI investment. During the 1950s–1970s when newly independent countries like Korea began her developmental efforts, international economic environment was not very friendly to FDI flow in general. Moreover, it turns out that FDI flows were very sensitive to resource endowments and domestic market size of the recipient countries. With its limited natural-resources and small domestic market, Korea at the time had little choice but to rely more on foreign borrowings, while the late-comer countries like China, India and Malaysia that are resource-rich and have potentially bigger market size under the more FDI-friendly international economic environment tend to rely relatively more on FDI. Singapore, Hong Kong and Dubai are special cases who positioned themselves for FDI as a strategic instrument for development by maximally utilizing their geopolitical and locational advantages and by providing a regulation-free economic environment.

References

Clark, Gregory. 2007. *A Farewell to Alms: A Brief Economic History of the World*. Princeton, NJ: Princeton University Press.

Drucker, Peter. 1993. *Post-Capitalist Society*. New York: Harper Business, a Division of HarperCollins Publishers.

Henrekson, Magnus, and Jakobsson Ulf. 2001. Where Schumpeter was Nearly Right—The Swedish Model and Capitalism, Socialism and Democracy. *Journal of Evolutionary Economics* 11 (3): 331–358.

Jwa, Sung-Hee. 2017. *A General Theory of Economic Development: Towards A Capitalist Manifesto*. Cheltenham: Edward Elgar.

North, Douglass. 1990. *Institutions, Institutional Change and Economic Performance*. Cambridge: Cambridge University Press.

North, Douglass, and Robert P. Thomas. 1973. *The Rise of the Western World*. Cambridge: Cambridge University Press.

North, Douglass, and Barry R. Weingast. 1989. Constitution and Commitment: The Evolution of Institutions Governing Public Choice in Seventeenth-Century England. *The Journal of Economic History* 49 (4): 803–832.

Schumpeter, Joseph. 1942. *Capitalism, Socialism, and Democracy, Harper Torchbooks, The University Library*. New York: Harper & Row Publishers.

CHAPTER 6

Korea's Economic Development

Abstract This chapter traces in details the economic evolution of Korea from the very early times to the present. The author explains how Korea's developmental era in the 1960s to 1980s was characterized by strong economic discrimination led by President Park Chung Hee. The chapter discusses in some details also Korea's macroeconomic management as well as corporate policies during the developmental era as well as in the post-"economic democratization" era in late-1980s under various regimes up to the 2000s, over which time economic and social policies have increasingly been influenced by egalitarianism. The 1997–1998 Asian financial crisis when Korea faced unprecedented economic woes and its aftermath are also treated in details.

Keywords Pre- and post-Park Chung Hee era
Government-led discrimination · Egalitarian trap
Economic democratization · Financial crisis · Economic discrimination by market, government and corporation

Economic Stagnation in Late-Chosun Dynasty

The old Korea under the monarchy system had suffered from desperate economic conditions that were hardly conducive to economic development; there was practically no individual economic freedom, no private property rights system, and the general education system was

S.-H. Jwa, *The Rise and Fall of Korea's Economic Development*,
DOI 10.1007/978-3-319-58065-4_6

poor. Important institutional bases for a market economy were largely absent. Korea's private property rights system was formally introduced only in 1912 under Japanese colonial rule following their system of intellectual property rights protection. Korean society was under a strict social caste system in the order of scholar-farmer-artisan-merchant; this is hardly conducive to economic progress. Towards the end of the 19th century in the late-Chosun dynasty, because of heavy taxes and exploitation by the widely-corrupted government officials, many Koreans migrated to the eastern tip of Russia where at least some early form of individual property rights protection had been institutionalized.[1] In the old Korea, there was an absence of any concept for a development-friendly government. In the words of Acemoglu et al. (2012), the Chosun dynasty was simply an extractor of people's properties and economic achievements. Government did not help those who help themselves, but rather exploited them for a long time. Pre-modern era in Korea can be described as strong government-led anti-economic discriminatory regime. We will return to this issue in Chap. 7.

Given her past, Korea is a very curious case of the developmental experiment in the modern era. Moreover, one can further ask, "Why are North and South Korea so radically different in their economic achievement?" Why is North Korea performing so poorly despite the fact that its people are identical to those of the South and it had started either at a similar or better condition than the South? Note that the economic institutional environment in modern North Korea today is not any better than that in the late-Chosun dynasty, and could be considered much worse, in fact. North Korea is an absolutely development-unfriendly nation under absolute exploitive egalitarian ideology and policies with no protection for economic freedom and private property rights. On top of that, government as well as leadership have absolutely no sense and willingness of motivating and leading the people and the economy towards progress. North Korea is probably the only society in the world where there exists absolutely no incentive to grow.

A New Interpretation of Korea's Modernization

Korea was established in 1948 following the end of WWII. President Rhee Syngman (1948–1960) led the adoption of liberal democracy and capitalist market economy on the US system. Universal suffrage was introduced together with various important market-friendly institutions, such as private property right (PPR) system and compulsory primary

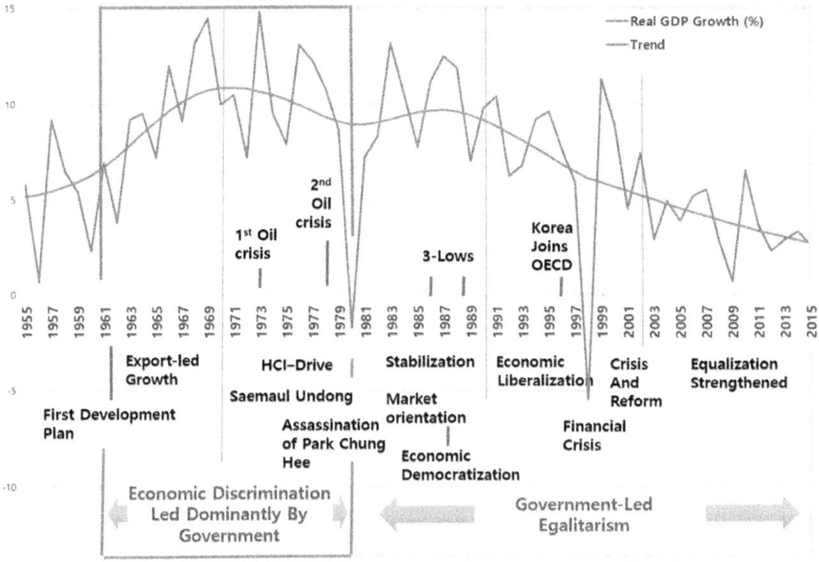

Fig. 6.1 Korea's long-term growth trend. *Source* The Bank of Korea

education. A sweeping land reform took place from March to May 1950, allowing the buying and selling of farmlands, while in North Korea land reform was based on a system of "confiscation without compensation and distribution free of charge under a collective farming system". However, even with the market system introduced, the Korean economy had yet to make marked improvement in her economy for almost 15 years, to make matters worse, in the midst of the interruption of the Korean War (1950–1953). The newly introduced market system needed a catalyst to help the economic take-off.

Korea achieved unprecedented high growth rates from the early 1960s for about 30 years. Thereafter the economy faced a steadily declining downward trend of growth potential extending another 30 years beginning from the late-1980s (see Fig. 6.1). What was the cause of the upward then downward trend in Korea's economy in the past 60 years? This section scrutinizes Korea's economic policy management experiences over the past 60 years under the new theoretical framework of development economics.

According to the new development economics perspective, during the so-called developmental era of the early 1960s and 1970s, the economic discrimination (ED) stance dominantly led by the government, which we have referred to as government-led economic discrimination of helping those who help themselves had been the key success factor for economic take-off and progress. Government support was always differentiated, based on the market performances. The incentive system in place was firmly based on the principle of economic discrimination that motivated Koreans and corporations to work harder. Under the strong development-oriented leadership of the late President Park Chung Hee, much of the political distortion that could interrupt the economic discrimination incentive system was greatly minimized.

However, the Post-Park era, especially since the late-1980s, forced the economic discrimination policy paradigm to gradually fade out, replaced by political populism which crept into the economic policy making sphere that resulted in the trend towards economic stagnation. The government began to push egalitarianism in all arenas as is evident in the economic and industrial policies, corporate policies, regional development policies, education policies, and industrial-relation policies. This is the era of economic democratization or growing social democracy during which the economic discrimination principle in government economic machinery has been overturned and economic dynamism was sacrificed.

A more detailed version of the Korea's 60 years economic development experiences follows.

Developmental Era from the 1960 to 1980 Under Government-Led Economic Discrimination (ED) Policy Regime

The history of Korea's modernization and rapid growth, at least prior to the early 1980s, is well-documented. In particular, widespread curiosity concerning Korea's "economic miracle" that followed near total devastation of the country during the Korean War has sparked a great deal of research interest in Korea and the Korean economy. In the early 1960s, following the inauguration of Park Chung Hee as the national leader and the launching of the Five-Year Development Plans, Korea recorded rapid growth, unprecedented in any other part of the world. The national development efforts such as the switch from import substitution to the export-led growth, the Saemaul Undong or New Village Movement, and the selective industrialization policy under the HCI (Heavy and Chemical Industry) drive are just a few of the many distinct policies responsible for Korea's rapid growth and development. Strong government intervention and guidance underlines the policy initiatives of Korea under Park Chung Hee.

Instead of documenting and describing the contents of individual policies, the discussion that follows explains what the success principle of the developmental era was from the perspective of the new development economics theory.

Economic Development Policies Consistent with Economic Discrimination (ED) Principle

The growth of the Korean economy in the 1960s and 1970s has been attributed to various factors. It is important nonetheless to note that the role of the government under the Park Chung Hee regime has been critical, acting as the main vehicle through which economically viable entities were selected and provided support, while those that were not deemed viable were removed from continued economic participation. Such "government-led economic discrimination" policies were based on explicit performance and capacity criteria.

For example, Korea's export promotion policy consistently rewarded the best export performers with tax and credit support. To strengthen the incentive system for export promotion, the government also established key administrative support systems. At the end of each month, the Export Promotion Committee headed by the President reviewed export progress and prepared necessary measures toward export targets. Furthermore, at the year-end export day ceremony on November 31st, led by the President himself, the government hosted the "export contest" to select the best export performers for further support; economic discrimination policies were at the center of the export and economic growth strategy.

With regard to industrial policy, specifically the promotion of heavy and chemical industry (HCI), the government maintained the same economically discriminatory policy mechanism by helping those firms that exhibited higher economic performances. Firms that demonstrated international competitiveness in their export activities by earning more dollars in the export promotion stage were allowed to enter the HCI sector with various government supports, thereby increasing the success probability of the nations' industrial policy. Korean industrial policy turns out to be a rare success case amongst 20th century history of industrial policy experiences in the world, thanks to "government-led economically discriminatory industrial policy".

As regards the Small and Medium Enterprise (SME) promotion policy, the government had also embedded economic discrimination in its support system by allowing higher market performers easier access to bank credit and the rights to acquire less performing SMEs often through government-led restructuring. As a result, a number of SMEs established in the 1950s and 1960s grew into big corporations in the 1980s and are now internationally competitive conglomerates like Samsung, Hyundai and LG.

ED was not confined to industry and business. In the rural areas, under the Saemaul Undong (New Village Movement) in the 1970s which intended to reform the mindset of the farmers and fishermen to become more development-friendly, the Ministry of Home Affairs classified all villages in the country on the basis of performance and level of development. The three categories were: 1. basic (underdeveloped) village, 2. self-help (developing) village, and 3. self-sufficient (developed) village. The government then adopted a highly discriminatory approach for each class of villages, giving higher assistance (not lower assistance) to higher-level villages—i.e. "government-led economic discrimination" policy again. Government support went to those villages that delivered better outcomes, while poorly performing ones were left out. This spurred competition among villages, particularly stimulating those in the lower classes to exert more effort towards advancing themselves to a higher level village so they may be eligible for government assistance. In this way, economic discrimination policy helped transform social reform policy like the Saemaul Undong into a development policy.

Moreover, given that Korea has strong Confucian ethos that tends to stress egalitarianism, it may be somewhat surprising that such a highly discriminatory policy, which proved to be very decisive in placing competitive entrepreneurs and firms into the forefront of Korea's economy as well as transforming the rural areas, managed to establish itself as the main mechanism driving Korea's economic transformation.[2]

Macroeconomic Policies Under Economic Discrimination Principle

Macroeconomic policies were also actively utilized to support the economically discriminatory growth and development policies. During the developmental era, there was always excess demand for credit and hence strong pressure for expansionary monetary policy under the national campaign to promote exports and produce economic growth. However, credit allocation by commercial banks usually followed the principle of economic discrimination; "banks always helped those firms who helped themselves", of course under the government's guidance.[3] This government-controlled banking system helped channel scarce credit to the most productive users, helping to minimize the inflationary pressure from increasing money supply. But of course, such a system could not completely avoid some typical inefficiencies of controlled banking. Also, when it came to fiscal policy, the main concern was to support industrial policy, rural development and infrastructure development projects, all for the sake of economic growth. In the end, however, during the developmental era, Korea was able to achieve high growth rates while containing the inflation rate within a relatively manageable range (average annual CPI inflation rate was 14.1% from 1966 to 1979) under the Park Chung Hee's regime.

Regarding exchange rate management, Korea in the 1960s and 1970s adopted a pegged exchange rate system under tight capital flow control, and managed exchange rates mostly in order not to harm export competiveness by correcting the overvaluation of the Korean won during the previous government and by keeping the won relatively competitive thereafter. The early correction of overvaluation with the maintenance of a relatively competitive level of exchange rate thereafter seems to have greatly helped Korea's export growth.

It is interesting to observe that for this period, the central bank monetary policy, the commercial banks' credit allocation policy, fiscal policy and exchange rate policy were all geared towards promoting exports and economic growth beyond their macroeconomic stabilization function, and was relatively successful in helping promote exports and economic growth without seriously aggravating inflationary pressure. This was possible because the financial resource allocation strategy was strictly guided by economic discrimination, minimizing potential inefficiencies of government intervention and, as a result, the credit supply in domestic and foreign currencies through government-controlled money and banking and exchange markets were effectively and smoothly channeled into investments that increased real production and value. The government's subsidy allocation strategy was also guided by the discrimination principle and any potential inefficiency related to government intervention was again minimized.

However, towards the late 1970s, the second oil shock that rocked the global economy also hit the Korean economy which was highly dependent on imported oil. Korea's exports were more seriously and negatively affected, and the nation was beginning to succumb to rising inflationary pressure.

Korea's Economy in Post-park Era Under Egalitarian Trap

From 1980 onwards, Korea introduced various market liberalization policies, first as a reaction to the strong government-led economic discrimination intervention of the Park Chung Hee era, then later, in the 1990s, as a mechanism to speed up Korea's democratization, globalization and integration into the world economy. We observe, however, that Korea has increasingly tended towards populist politics by leaning on egalitarian principles under the various banners of democracy, market liberalization, and globalization—gradually at first then at an excessively rapid pace. As a result, much of Korea's public policy has lost many of the discriminating features that proved to be so decisive during the early stages of her modernization. Although some of the institutions and practices in economic management of the early modernization period still survive formally until today, the Korean economy has turned into a rather different character under the various ideologies of the past three decades, becoming increasingly influenced by egalitarian principles. In what follows, I attempt to trace this shift away from "government-led discrimination" to "government-led egalitarianism" of the past three decades by drawing, as clearly as possible, a broad panoramic picture of the Korean economy.[4]

The 1980s to the Early 1990s Sowed the Seed of Economic Egalitarianism

Korea entered the 1980s under the new political leadership of Chun Doo-hwan (1980–1987), who introduced the ideas of liberalization and stabilization into the public policy sphere largely as a reaction to the policies of the previous government. Despite consolidating Korea's industrial and corporate strength, the popular criticism at the time was that Park Chung Hee's industrialization and particularly the HCI drive had brought with it various structural problems of which the most notorious seems to have been over-investment, rapid unbalanced urbanization, high inflation, and increased government deficit. The international economic environment in the early 1980s, including the second oil shock and its aftermath, was also extremely hostile. The situation further restricted Korea's exports and encouraged the Chun Doo-hwan regime to concentrate on stabilization, especially to control inflation in its first two years. Tight monetary and fiscal policies were adopted at the macro level while attempting to bring about economic restructuring. Despite a negative growth rate and high political unrest in 1980 following the assassination of Park in 1979, the economy did rebound to attain 8.1%

growth rate by 1983. Exports recovered in mid-1983 and the economy began to gain its strength.[5]

At the beginning of the 1980s, the authorities were faced with the question of how to deal with the chaebol (Korea's large corporations, which grew rapidly during the 1960s and 1970s).[6] Two possible ways to address the so called "chaebol problem", or the perceived threat of economic concentration, would have been (1) a transition to a free-market economy in which the pressure of competition and the threat of bankruptcy would act as the major market disciplinary mechanism and (2) the use of various regulations on financing, investment and loan guarantees to control chaebol behavior and expansion. Authorities chose to rely primarily on the latter approach thereby limiting the role of Korea's large corporations, and this has had several negative consequences. For example, it called for considerable government intervention in the private sector's economic decision-making, which limited the role of market forces. As a result, moral hazard behavior became pervasive throughout the economy. Furthermore, the government in the early 1980s began promoting small- and medium-sized enterprises (SMEs) by establishing SME sanctuaries and by requiring banks to comply with a compulsory lending ratio program. In effect, the government's arbitrary decision to encourage SMEs came at the expense of large corporations. Moreover, there was no guarantee that SMEs could become competitive without adequate demand from large corporations because most of the former were parts and capital good suppliers for the latter. In fact, because of its negative impact on large firms, the decision to skew policy towards SMEs resulted in adversely affecting not only SMEs but also the overall national economy. It is worth noting here that given Korea's industrial organization structure led by the large assembly companies networked with SMEs supplying parts and capital goods, there has always been high dependence of SMEs on large corporations and vice versa. Simply put, directly regulating large corporations' business behavior may succeed in limiting their economic expansion, but repercussions to the economy as well as to SMEs cannot be avoided.[7] To influence chaebol behavior without destroying incentives for growth and expansion, the government would therefore have been better off strengthening competitive pressure on large corporations by augmenting and consolidating the country's competition promotion policy. That is, by inviting more potential as well as actual competitors, chaebols' incentive to abuse its economic power could have been reduced.

Not unrelated to chaebol regulation, the government adopted a balanced regional development policy in 1982 which began to regulate the 30 largest chaebols' investment in the Seoul-Gyeonggi metropolitan region. This was intended to divert resources to help the remaining local regions grow, thereby attaining balanced development. However, because of the restrictions to invest in the metropolitan city areas where competitive advantage in terms of capital and manpower supplies were available, large corporations decided rather to move investment out of Korea for their investment. For the past 40 years, this balanced regional development policy has failed miserably in achieving its intended policy goals but has still not been revoked.

Between 1985 (the year of the Plaza Accord) and 1988 (the year of the Seoul Summer Olympics), economic conditions favored strong economic growth, in what has been called the "three lows" period (1986–1988), characterized by the low value of the dollar and the won relative to the yen, low oil prices, and low international interest rates. The rise in foreign demand, a relatively low won, low inflation, and an industrial structure already geared to exports thanks to the successful construction of the heavy and chemical industry (HCI) created an export boom for Korea, thus helping to generate current account surplus (more than 5% of GDP in 1988). The stabilization efforts succeeded in keeping inflation low while allowing double-digit growth rates from 1986 to 1988.

Notwithstanding the successful macroeconomic stabilization by inflation control and booming exports at the time, the Chun Doo-hwan government did in fact pave the road for economic egalitarianism by introducing the egalitarian corporate policy of regulating chaebols and promoting SMEs uniformly as well as balanced regional development policy of regulating the growth of metropolitan-capital city region and promoting other regions uniformly under the populist banner of "social justice". These policies were adopted despite—or probably because of—the fact that the government itself was politically authoritarian having found itself in power following an unjustifiable military coup. Furthermore, it is interesting to see how the booming economy thanks to the "three lows" together with low inflation and with the already established HCI industrial base had given a somewhat wrong signal that the new egalitarian policy approach helped create the economic boom. From then on, Korea's economic policy landscape rapidly became more and more egalitarian without much hesitation. In this sense, the economic boom in the late-1980s has turned out to be a disguised curse for Korea.

After winning the 1987 December elections with just 37% of the votes, Roh Tae-woo was inaugurated as president in February 1998, and this has been credited as the first peaceful transfer of presidential power in South Korea's history. Roh quickly sought to accelerate political democratization and market liberalization. Furthermore, the constitutional reform in 1987 before his election, activated under the strong nation-wide pro-democracy movement and with the inclusion of "economic democratization" in the new constitution, has placed a definite mark on the break away from the government-led discrimination strategy of previous regimes. Specifically, the Korean Constitution formally introduced the concept of economic democracy with Article 119 on 29 October 1987. It states that first, "the economic order of the country should respect the economic freedom and creativity of individuals and of firms", which was introduced originally under the Park Chung Hee regime in December 1962 and kept in place with only minor revisions by adding "firms" in addition to individuals, and second, as a new addition, that "the government should regulate and coordinate the economy to achieve balanced economic growth and stability and fair income distribution, prevent monopoly market power and the abuse of economic power, as well as achieve 'economic democracy' by promoting economic harmony amongst different economic groups". The idea of economic democracy has had significant consequences. Korea's labor policy, for example, allowed for the strengthening of labor union's influence which favored wage increases; frequent and violent labor disputes increased, workers demanded greater involvement in management decisions, and the huge wage hikes (11% annually during 1989–1991) far exceeded the rise in productivity. While this seems to have occurred as a reaction to suppressed labor and human rights during the previous regimes, the force of this reaction was so strong that it shifted the pendulum too far to the left. Simultaneously, contrary to the general liberalization stance of the government, regulations on corporate activities and expansion of the large corporate sector were again strengthened.

The economic policies under the regime of Roh Tae-woo (1988–1992) largely driven by populist politics were often ill conceived and inconsistent. The full effect of policy mistakes were cushioned somewhat by the favorable "three lows" period, but eventually, high financial costs, excessive administrative regulations on business activities, and low social overhead capital investment were typical of the period, which gradually eroded industrial and firm competitiveness and entrepreneurship. The late 1980s saw Korea's export competitiveness deteriorate due to labor disputes, rising interest rates and a sharply appreciating won.[8] The US$ 8.8 billion trade surplus of 1988, one of the largest even by world standards, dwindled to practically nothing in 1989 and was followed by progressively larger deficits in the 1990s.[9]

Increasingly, technology became an important factor determining international competitiveness, and the disappointment of decades of policies trying to strengthen SMEs to provide high quality component parts at competitive prices started to become evident. However, despite the clear advantage of Korea's large corporations in gaining access to new markets and new technology, as well as in saving on production costs, the increasing public sentiment against the chaebol together with populist politics paved the way for an even stronger shift towards emphasizing SMEs and regulating chaebol behavior, a trend that continued under the Kim Young-Sam (1993–1997) and Kim Dae-jung (1998–2002) governments. It is interesting to note that the Korea Fair Trade Commission (KFTC),[10] established in 1981 to promote competition in the private sector, has in fact been a strong advocacy for SMEs and somewhat tended to adopt the singular goal of limiting chaebol activities and expansion. The crucial point is that the overall economy suffered as a result of the government's attempts to directly control economic concentration specifically by regulating chaebol investment behavior.[11] The KFTC should have stuck to its original function of enhancing competitive pressure on the corporate sector through properly implemented competition policy.

In sum, Korea's constitutional declaration in favor of economic democracy signaled formally the beginning of the government-led egalitarianism in policy making by actively favoring labor over capital, as well as the promotion of SMEs over large firms and local regions over Seoul metropolis area. The government aimed at equalizing the economic powers in the corporate ecosystem by restricting the business activities of large corporations and at the same time promoting SMEs. Labor unions became increasingly active as was seen by increasing demand for management democracy and stronger union militancy.

Causes of Financial Crisis in 1997–1998

Internationally, following the collapse of the Soviet bloc, the 1990s witnessed growing regionalization as economic trade blocs among countries of Europe and America were created. With the World Trade

Organization (WTO), a new regime in international trade was formed to increase pressure to liberalize previously protected markets particularly in agricultural goods and financial services. Kim Young-Sam's government (1993–1997) was quick to catch on and this time, on top of accelerated liberalization, announced segyehwa (globalization) as a priority national goal. The government's effort to gain international legitimacy culminated in Korea's accession to the OECD in 1996, which seemed to signal Korea's entry into the rank of advanced countries.

Populist politics again, but this time with a vengeance, characterized Kim Young-Sam, who decisively beat the main opposition party while campaigning on a platform promising reform of government controls and regulations. On his arrival into office, he immediately forced the disclosure of private assets of the public officeholders, expelled corrupt officials, called for the enactment of a law on officeholders' ethics, and introduced the "real name financial account system".[12] A closer look underneath the government's tearing down of old institutions and the embracing of "market principles" to lead economic reform reveals a somewhat different picture. In reality, under Korea's formal liberalization and deregulation measures, there has always been strong influence on the private sector by government.[13] Financial retardation continued under the "*kwanchi kumyung*" (government-controlled finance), while labor became increasingly militant and uncompromising as accelerated democratization impacted the economic sphere as well. The continued antagonism towards large corporations encouraged the government to put further pressure on the chaebol to comply with government rules and regulations. Under such a hostile environment, it is no wonder that the economy gradually lost their competitive edge in an increasingly competitive world economy.

In the 1990s prior to the Asian Financial crisis, apart from the deteriorating current account balance from 1994 onwards, Korea's macroeconomic picture in general looked rather positive. The opening up of the economy helped economic growth to rise from 3% in 1992 to 8.6 and 8.9% in 1994 and 1995, respectively. Exports and imports surged to record levels, but the overvaluation of the Korean won did little to cushion the growing current account deficit. Per capita income surpassed the US$ 10,000 mark in 1995, and in 1996 when Korea joined the OECD. The unemployment rate was also impressive, recorded at an unprecedented 2%. Notwithstanding the high economic growth, inflation remained relatively stable at a 4% level throughout most of the 1990s.

Causes and problems of the 1997 financial crisis can be summarized as follows. First, behind this "healthy" macroeconomic picture was an overvalued exchange rate maintained partly to keep Korea's per capita income above the US$ 10,000 mark—a requirement to join the OECD.[14] Overvaluation of the exchange rate was even successful to the extent of having helped inflation stay at low levels despite the drastic wage hikes. However, Korea's corporate competitiveness throughout most of the 1990s declined as a result of exchange rate overvaluation, high domestic interest rates, high wage increases, increasing labor disputes, and some inefficient investments.[15] Second, not only the speed but also the sequencing of liberalization resulted in economic problems. Specifically, given the high domestic interest rates, the liberalization of controls on short-term capital before long-term capital encouraged banks to back long-term domestic lending with short-term foreign borrowing, which left them vulnerable to foreign interest spikes, domestic currency depreciation or a creditors' panic.[16] Third, further policy mistakes that were largely overlooked include an unsustainable foreign exchange reserve based on IMF estimates that were actually more relevant for a non-liberalized capital and foreign exchange system. A reserve of 3 month worth of imports was recommended to keep the balance of payments stable, which proved to be insufficient under liberalized capital flow and rigid exchange rates. The foreign exchange reserve quickly dried up in a couple of months as the government tried to cushion the effects of a falling won towards the end of 1997. Fourth, a narrow and immature financial system remained under the pervasive pattern of government intervention. With prudential regulations not strictly abided to, upon full liberalization and opening up of the country's financial markets, the financial system became increasingly exposed to all sorts of vulnerabilities. Finally, the government's futile effort to defend the overvalued won against market expectation expedited capital flight and helped deplete foreign exchange stocks.

In fact, Korea's financial crisis is a typical case of policy coordination failure. The Korean government aimed at keeping the Korean won strong due to the political consideration of meeting the OECD requirements and money supply relatively tight for inflation control before the outbreak of the crisis, which proved to have been an inappropriate policy mix because the real sector, heavily dependent on exports, lost export price competitiveness due to the strong won. The situation was further aggravated by high factor costs such as the high domestic interest rate and high wage rates. Strong anti-inflationary policies with overvaluation of the Korean won and a tight money supply, especially in 1997 when the Korean economy was experiencing the worst cyclical downturn since the early 1970s, hit businesses already in weak financial positions, thereby having created a series of potentially insolvent mid-sized large corporations. The weakened economy could not stand this policy stance, becoming particularly vulnerable to adverse shocks. However, the situation had continued on without any decisive policy actions to restructure those corporations subject to default risk as well as without any corrective macroeconomic policy measures to break through the overall policy stalemate.

This was soon apparent to foreign investors who, on witnessing this sequence of events and the weakening economy, began to rapidly pull out their Korean holdings. The optimal policy mix under the mounting pressure of capital flight near the outbreak of crisis would have been to allow the immediate depreciation of the Korean won reflecting the market expectation, while the actual policy turned out to resist the depreciation of the Korean won even to the point of depletion of foreign exchange reserve, thus contributing to the collapse into the financial crisis in late 1997.

In hindsight, the most important policy mistake leading to the financial crisis was the exchange rate policy to overvalue the Korean won and to try to defend the overvalued rate until the last minute of reserve depletion.[17] On October 1997, the Korean Stock Exchange began to plunge followed by a sharp fall of the Korean won against dollar.[18] The depreciation of the won exerted inflationary pressure, which shot up to an average of 7.5% in 1998 (compared to 4.5% in 1997 and 0.8% in 1999). By November 21, Korea's foreign reserves were nearly depleted, and to prevent the total insolvency of the economy, the government announced that it would seek emergency loan from the International Monetary Fund (IMF) to overcome the difficulties in the financial and currency markets. The Korean government and the IMF agreed on November 21 on IMF emergency rescue loans of 21 billion US$. Later on December 3, the total credit line increased to US$ 55 billion with the addition of US$ 10 billion by the World Bank, US$ 4 billion by the ADB and US$ 20 billion by 7 major countries including the US, Japan and Germany. In return for this loan, Korea was put under the so-called IMF reform program in 4 areas: public sector, corporate sector, financial sector and labor sector.[19] Kim Dae-jung, who was just elected president

(1998–2002) on his fourth attempt, was suddenly to face the most devastating economic hardship Korea would experience since the Korean War.

Travelling Through Financial Crisis

The IMF recommended extremely tight fiscal and monetary policies in the very early stage of crisis management as a part of the overall stabilization program. Faced with the prospects of a significant negative turnaround in the overall budget deficit stemming from reduced tax revenue and interest costs of government borrowing to bail out the insolvent banks for financial sector restructuring, fiscal balance was sought as the initial target of the fiscal policy. According to consultations with the IMF, the Korean government introduced measures to increase excise and oil taxation, expand the tax base, freeze civil service salaries and reduce current expenditures.

To limit capital flight, the IMF plan assumed that the resultant high interest rates by adopting a tight monetary stance would induce capital inflow while increasing the cost of capital flight, and thereby reduce the pressure on the foreign exchange market. The belief was that if left unchecked, exchange rate overshooting would trigger a depreciation-inflation spiral. The continued depreciation could impose substantial burdens on both the corporate and banking sectors, which were already suffering from overexposure to foreign-currency-denominated liabilities. This follows the more traditional way of handling exchange market overshooting by keeping interest rates high for several months and later easing the tight monetary policy in line with foreign exchange market stabilization. Nonetheless, there was a growing concern among critics including this author[20] of the IMF plan over the rising interest rates, as it was not effective in stabilizing the foreign exchange market. They argued that since the Korean government controlled capital outflow reasonably well and the Korean bond market had negligible foreign investment, tighter monetary policy and higher interest rates would have a minimal positive effect of bringing in capital inflow, while further demolishing the already devastated business sector. Indeed, the higher interest rates and large scale restructuring of the financial sector under the direction of the government resulted in a credit crunch that drove many businesses into bankruptcy. Social disruption increased as the unemployment rate more than doubled from 2.6% in 1997 to 6.8% in 1998.

In early 1998, acknowledging the various problems with the IMF package, the government reversed its policy stance and eased monetary policy and expanded fiscal spending. Market pressure on the won had somewhat eased following successful informal negotiations for a standstill on short-term debt, and the won began to strengthen gradually, stabilizing at around the 1300 won per dollar by August 1998 from the record high 1965 won per dollar in the year-end of 1997. The successful rescheduling of short-term debt of more than US$ 21 billion, completed in April, was an important factor behind improved currency stability. Usable foreign reserves, having shrunk to less than US$ 9 billion, increased to more than US$ 30 billion by April, surpassing the pre-crisis level, and continued to increase to reach US$ 52 billion by yearend, largely helped on by the significantly improved current account position under the historically low won, amounting to US$ 40.4 billion at the year-end of 1998 rapidly turning around from the US$ 23.1 billion deficit in 1997. Ironically, most of this current account surplus was earned by the large exporting chaebols which were in fact blamed and scapegoated as causing the crisis by borrowing too much and put to the strict reform program.[21]

The high interest rate policy was gradually eased in parallel with the improved currency stability. The call rate fell to 14–15% by June, down from 22% in March. (The overnight call rate had once peaked at about 35% in early January 1998.) The high interest rates had already caused quite a bit of damage by creating an additional burden on debt servicing of the banks and the corporate firms. Furthermore, Korean banks had to reduce their loan portfolios to meet the 8% BIS capital ratio, which together with the already severe credit crunch resulted in contraction in the real sector.

The Korean government also changed the direction of its fiscal policy and started to put greater emphasis on providing fiscal stimulus. Since the interest rate policy was more concerned with currency stability, fiscal policy had to play a greater role in stimulating domestic demand and in providing some kind of safety net. In May 1998, the targeted budget deficit for the year was adjusted upward to 1.7% of GDP. Following a sharp fall in output and amid increasing social pressures, the government shifted gears by introducing further stimulus focused on deficit spending comprising 5% of GDP in July. At the same time, the mobilization of public funds of about 64 trillion won (approximately US$ 45 billion) was allocated to financial restructuring, which was again augmented later in 2000 by another 40 trillion won. Government-led restructuring in the financial sector as well as the corporate sector, which encouraged the wholesale adoption of so-called "global standards", slowly precipitated into "reform fatigue"[22] by the end of 2000. Moreover, a substantial burden has now been placed on public finance—for example, government debt in 2000 was 40% of GDP, and with financial and corporate restructuring still in progress, debt continued to rise.

In 1999 and 2000, the spectacular export growth and rebound in domestic consumption and investment in Korea has helped push the unpleasant memories of the crisis years into the background. GDP growth registered 10.9% in 1999 and 9.3% in 2000. The exchange rate had stabilized somewhat at around 1200 won to the dollar and the stock market has remained more or less healthy during this period. Current account surpluses and foreign exchange reserves provide ample cover against short-term maturing liabilities. For example, in 2001, the foreign exchange reserves at the end of March stood at US$94.4 billion, roughly sufficient for about 6 months of imports (and which compares closely with the US$93.34 billion, US$94.53 billion, and US$96.2 billion in total reserves at the end of October, November, and December in 2000, respectively). Foreign exchange outflows were more than matched by inflows every month of 2001.

With this background of continuously improving current account surpluses and reserve position from 1998 and on, the President Kim Dae-jung was able to declare the end of the crisis on November 19, 1999, and Korea was able to pay back all the rescue loans by August 23, 2001.

Destroying Incentives for Growth and Expansion

It is also interesting to note that the Kim Dae-jung government at the outbreak of the financial crisis immediately put in place what are called chaebol reform policies that demanded corporate restructuring by way of increased management transparency, elimination of cross-debt guarantees, strengthening accountability to shareholders, reduced debt-equity ratios and specialization to "core" business lines under the IMF reform program as one of the conditions of the IMF rescue loan. Furthermore, the anti-chaebol reform policies were in fact strengthened in the midst of the crisis when fingers were pointed at the chaebol for causing the crisis with over-borrowing and by letting the second largest chaebol as well as the best exporting corporation, Daewoo Corp, to go bankrupt in 1999 under the tight export credit crunch led partly by the government. More than a dozen mid-sized chaebols dissolved in the crisis via the restructuring process.

Although such measures for chaebol restructuring have been officially credited to have helped Korea regain international competitiveness, they still fall short of satisfactorily explaining the quick economic recovery. It would seem that macroeconomic corrective measures rather than structural reform should be credited for resolving a bulk of the problems of the 1997 crisis, the latter usually requiring a longer period of time to take shape as well as to realize the effects of such reforms. In fact, it is hard in principle to blame the chaebols for the crisis and to attribute the quick recovery to the chaebol reform measures because they were in large part the victims of policy mistakes. In hindsight, the chaebol reforms during the crisis signaled the end of the Park Chung Hee's growth paradigm or government-led economic discrimination, thereby destroying to a large extent the incentive for growth of the corporate sector. Ever since then it had become harder to expect and see in the Korean economy examples of past dynamic creative entrepreneurs as witnessed so rampantly during the developmental era and the growth trend of the corporate sector has rapidly slowed down as seen in the figures on the corporate sector in Appendix 1.

Economic Policy Increasingly Turning into Egalitarian Policy

Since the financial crisis, Korea has experienced worsening growth and distribution following the short-lived rebound immediately after the crisis. With this background, entering the mid-2000s, social policy concerns began to dominate the public debate while growth and development policy issues have increasingly lost sight of economic discrimination, which has been overwhelmed by strengthening egalitarian ethos and policy. Social policy by its nature is often intertwined with egalitarianism, which of course explains why the welfare system based on the political promise of equal income for all such as the European welfare system cannot be sustainable. Currently, Korea's welfare policy is increasingly adopting the nonperforming, egalitarian support system and the nation's growth and development policies has followed suit without much reflection or discourse. It is interesting to see that growth and development policy has become nominal and in fact has turned into a kind of social policy in substance.

This trend has been reinforced by most of the latter governments, the leftwing Roh Moo-hyun government (2003–2007), the rightwing Lee Myung-Bak government (2008–2012), the rightwing Park Geun-Hye government (2013–2016), and the newly inaugurated leftwing

Moon Jae-In government (2017–); regardless of their ideological difference, the general economic policy direction of Korea is now firmly in the hands of economic egalitarianism. Currently, Korea has adopted increasingly egalitarian economic institutions and policies under the populist pressure for "economic democracy", which has survived for quarter a century and has gained even more steam recently, thereby shaping economic policy to become more egalitarian ever since the post-Park Chung Hee era up until the present day. Consequently, the Korean people's self-help spirit that was a decisive factor for the Korean miracle in the developmental era has been substituted by the "blame-it-on-the-others" mentality. Needless to say, Korean growth rates have turned out disappointing as well, as seen in Fig. 6.1.

Evaluation of Post-park Era

We have explained how from the late-1980s onwards, the nature of Korea's economic policy framework has changed tremendously under the banners of liberalization, democracy and globalization. Gradually at first and then rapidly, governments after Park Chung Hee took on an increasingly liberal and mainly populist flavor. Specifically, egalitarian motives seem to have molded into what I call a "government-led egalitarian policy" framework, which often goes against the national objectives of introducing market principles, and which is also sharply differentiated with the "government-led discrimination" mechanism. We observe that Korea has increasingly lost many of the discriminating features that proved to be so decisive during the early stages of her industrialization. With Korea's economic policy framework increasingly under the influence of egalitarian principles, it has transformed away from "government-led discrimination" to "government-led egalitarianism" in which most economic policies that should have been discriminating were turned into a kind of social policy which lacked incentive differentiation.

With the shift of political power from the administrative body to the national assembly, populist politics has become even more dominating over economic policy making, thereby adversely affecting Korea's economic dynamism. This is totally in the opposite direction to the situation under President Park's regime in which economic concerns dominated political considerations. Despite the commitment to introduce and develop markets on the surface, in reality, economic decisions remain largely at the discretion of the politicians who tend to favor egalitarianism mainly for their own vote-maximization purposes. Even worse, they are left unattended simply because politicians as well as government officials cannot possibly handle all issues as effectively as before in an increasingly complex economy. And as we have mentioned, efforts at handling corporate issues, in particular economic concentration, have wrongly relied on direct regulation rather than through enhancing competitive pressure. The policy dichotomy between large corporations on the one hand and SMEs on the other was mostly founded on political grounds to maximize votes, which has carried with it adverse economic consequences as policy inclined to favor the latter usually at the expense of the former. Rather, a more holistic perspective would have been preferable—one that exerts competitive pressure on large firms by inviting more competitors, actual as well as potential. Large corporations under strong competitive pressure would then seek cooperation and strengthened relations with parts-supplying SMEs, which would ultimately be beneficial for mutual success and survival, resulting in sustained economic growth. We will return to this issue in the next section.

Industrial policy and government policies to develop the national economy have been pursued by all nations in modern history. Yet some countries have failed while others have succeeded. Korea belongs to the fortunate group of countries where her industrial policy, particularly, in the 1960s and 1970s, can be credited to have generated unprecedented economic growth and development. That notwithstanding, in general, public policy including those addressing economic issues became contaminated by egalitarian ethos and principles, following the country's transition to democracy in 1987. This "government-led egalitarianism" in many ways tended to favor the economically nonviable entities by reverse-discriminating stronger and more viable entities in terms of government support and regulation.

In sum, for the past 30 years or so, Korea has been trapped in egalitarian reforms that aim to "equalize the starting point for all", thereby disfavoring the large, rich, and prospering people, organizations, corporations, schools and regions, and so on, in favor of the smaller, weaker, poorer and stagnating entities. The most critical damage resulting from the government-led egalitarian policy has been to destroy the very incentives for individuals as well as corporations to grow and expand because it tends to penalized growing and high performing economic agents. Specific examples of the egalitarian trap since 1987 are as follows: 1. The regulation of large corporations to achieve a balanced corporate sector because they were perceived as too big and becoming a stumbling block to economic democracy, 2. Support for SMEs because they are smaller and weaker, and not because they are more efficient, thereby reverse-discriminating against the relatively better performing SMEs, 3. Distribution of R&D funds favorably to the weaker firms in an egalitarian manner, thereby reverse-discriminating against stronger R&D performing firms, 4. Distribution of research funds not strictly based on the performance but rather on egalitarian consideration, 5. Support for farmers because they are lagging-behind, not because of improved economic performance, which is totally opposite to the spirit of the Saemaul Undong (see Chap. 7), 6. Regulation of metropolitan regions by banning large corporations' investments and the new establishment or expansion of 4-year universities, while unreservedly supporting all localities equally to achieve balanced regional development, 7. Disfavoring Seoul metropolitan universities but favoring regional universities for balanced growth among universities and regions, 8. Introduction of an educational system that is aimed at equalizing students' performances across schools and regions, and 9. A drastic rise in labor unions' militancy as well as the demands for management democracy[23] in the name of compensating labor's supposedly weak position and suppression during the industrialization process,[24] which put enormous pressure on corporate activities thereby hampering the country's industrial competitiveness.

All the above policies contributed to the 1997/1998 economic crisis. But this should not be surprising if we recognize that "government-led egalitarianism" under the guise of "economic democracy", if taken to the extreme, is hardly different from socialism, and as history reveals, socialism itself is largely based on egalitarian principles, which contain serious contradictions that are incompatible with sustainable economic growth and development.

Be that as it may, under the egalitarian trap, Korea's economy has not performed as it did in the earlier stages of economic development when it was guided by economic discrimination policy. As shown in Fig. 6.1, the long-term growth trend of the Korean economy has been continuously declining ever since the late 1980s.

Suggestions for the Future of Korea

The arguments above notwithstanding, Korea cannot revert back wholly to and solely rely on the economic discrimination mechanism led dominantly by the government among the holy trinity of development

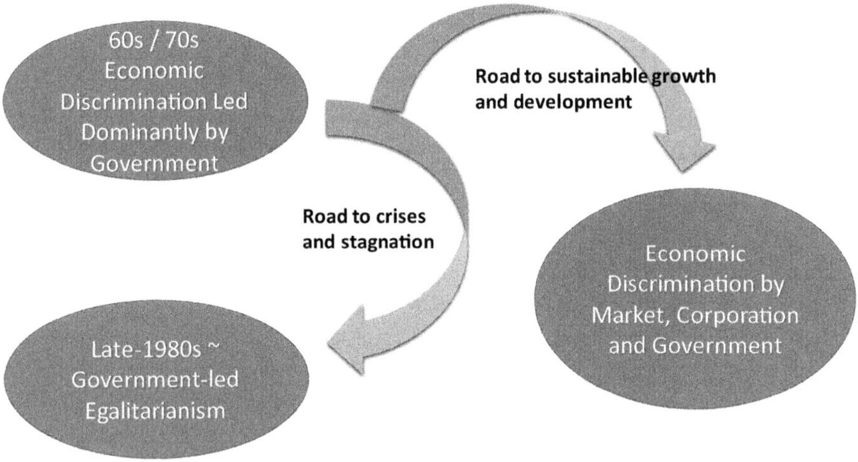

Fig. 6.2 Korea's path to sustainable economic growth

(see Fig. 6.2). In principle, it has been argued that the government-led development strategy can suffer potentially from various side-effects, for example: (1) unfair opportunities arising from government's unfair discretion, (2) corruption in the form of illegal government-business interlocking practices including kick-backs and bribery, and (3) moral hazard behavior on the part of private agents under government support.

Park's developmental era, however, had been relatively free from such adverse effects because economic discrimination policy was geared towards creating stiff domestic competition and dynamism among corporations. Moreover, it is generally acknowledged that Park was a leader free from corruption. In the post-Park era however many side-effects began to crop up under "misguided" government intervention that lacked economic discrimination. Be that as it may, the creation of chaebols itself during the Park's regime as well as such negative side effects under various governments have fueled the widespread anti-corporate sentiment (or anti-chaebol sentiment) among the general public, as the growth of large corporations were increasingly perceived as an outcome of unfair government support.

Going forward, the economic discrimination mechanism led by the holy trinity of development, market, corporation and government rather than the egalitarian hand of the government, is what will be required for Korea's sustainable economic development (see Fig. 6.2). The role of the government needs to move away from direct intervention void of economic discrimination to the building of institutions that embody economic discrimination for the effective discrimination functioning of markets. There is need therefore to promote and upgrade the "market-led discrimination" in tandem with "government-led discrimination" that augments the markets whenever "market-led discrimination" turns out to be weak, while at the same time taking caution to avoid 'government-led egalitarianism'. This in fact should be the guiding mechanism for Korea's future economic development. The government must introduce and maintain market discrimination-conforming institutions that help those who help themselves, including the provision of individual economic freedom, private property rights protection, fair and just legal system, competition promotion policy, as well as the promotion of discrimination function of the financial institutions and markets, while abandoning egalitarianism, thereby reviving the discriminatory function of economic policies.

And together with markets and the government, we must not forget to nurture the growth of corporations as important players in the development process. As we have already mentioned, corporations are an essential part of the puzzle of economic development, functioning and also exercising economic discrimination in an economic environment under market- and the government-led discrimination. In this respect, one of the most important and thorniest policy issues in Korea is the chaebol regulation policy. There is still much confusion and need for serious institutional reform. The Korean economy critically depends upon the fate of corporations, or the chaebols, whether or not they are at all favorably received by the Korean society. This is the dilemma faced by Koreans because the Korean economy is unsustainable without the chaebol but the government seems to shy away from policies that fairly treat the chaebol (not even to the levels of favor that they are prepared to extend to foreign corporations) because some opinions continue to strongly argue for the "correction" of the wrongful past favors to the chaebol. This contradicts the new economic development perspective which implies that corporations and the chaebols in particular are a necessary feature of Korea's economic development.[25] Instead, what has transpired is reverse-discrimination vis-à-vis foreign, FDI competitors as well as domestic SMEs, which is very unfortunate. As we have reviewed above, the Korean economy has been losing dynamism all along with increasing regulations on the chaebols' economic activities under the egalitarian policy regime driven by "economic democracy" while the government or political leadership seems to have no political power or will to change the existing regulatory regime under the current social-political pressure from anti-chaebol sentiment. Korea may lose her chance to recover diminished incentives for growth and may continue her desperate journey along the zero-growth path unless there is some genuine change in the current policy stalemate. An alternative policy paradigm toward chaebol regulation is in dire need.

The main message to keep in mind may be summarized as, "Care should be taken not to confuse ability with incentives to abuse economic power."[26] Public policy should refrain from trying to contain the apparent threat of conglomeration in ways that destroy incentives for growth. The threat of market power can be efficiently tackled by allowing stronger competitive pressure of potential as well as actual rivals while government-protected monopolies should always be avoided. However, there has been much confusion between ability and incentives to abuse economic power, leading the government to directly regulate ability by limiting corporate growth activities thereby destroying incentives for growth and expansion. This is the key reason for the continuously declining growth dynamism we have experienced over the years. The new policy paradigm for chaebol regulation to revive Korea's growth dynamism is to put those existing chaebols under steep competition by allowing actual as well as potential competition among themselves and from FDI as well as by encouraging the SMEs to grow into larger corporations through transforming the existing egalitarian into economically discriminatory, SME promotion policy. Such a policy paradigm can contain the incentive to abuse while at the same time help revive the incentives for growth and expansion. Otherwise, it may be impossible for Korea to escape from the side-effects of strong government egalitarian intervention as mentioned earlier as well as from the low growth trap.

Furthermore, in the same vein, it is necessary to bring the economic discrimination incentive mechanism into social empowerment policies including social safety-net policies as well to create incentives for growth on the part of the policy beneficiaries and thereby enhance sustainability because the economic discrimination incentive mechanism will help align social policies with growth and development in the broader sense. So far, social policy has been subdued by egalitarian ethos and has therefore become unsustainable in many cases because egalitarian policy removes the very incentives to create value in favor of redistribution. Therefore, such social policy should be reformed to embody economic discrimination if sustainability is to be improved.[27]

To sum up, all types of growth and development policies in Korea need to recover its economic discriminatory function and even social empowerment policies could do well by incorporating economic discrimination in order to become self-sustainable. This is the main challenge for the Korean economy in the 21st century.

Notes

1. It turned out that Korean migrants were the best economically ahead of the Chinese and the Russians that lived in the neighborhood. Credit may go to the new institutional environment with individual property right system. See Isabella Bird Bishop (1970), "Korea and her neighbors" for further discussions.
2. The reason for this will be fully explained later in Chap. 7. As of now it may suffice to say that the leadership of Park Chung Hee was highly discriminatory, only helping those who help themselves. He always kept to discriminatory policies.
3. In fact, the economic discrimination in credit allocation is the fundamental loan screening function of the commercial banks but does not function well usually in the underdeveloped market system like in Korea under 1960s–1970s so that the government can help re-enforce the weak function of the bank's economic discrimination credit allocation for economic development.
4. The discussion will follow the chronically the Post-Park Korean governments' policies during 1980–2012: Chun Doo-hwan, 1980–1987; Roh Tae-woo, 1988–1992; Kim Young-Sam, 1993–1997; Kim Dae-jung, 1998–2002; Roh Moo-hyun, 2003–2007; Lee Myung-Bak, 2008–2012; Park Geun-Hae, 2013–2016; Moon Jae-In, 2017– (though the post-financial crisis governments from Roh Moo-hyun are very lightly touched upon).
5. The real GNP growth rate was 7% in 1985, but for the next 3 years 12.9, 12.8, and 12.2%, respectively.
6. See Jwa (2002b) for a comprehensive discussion on the issues of the Korean Chaebol. It is not an exaggeration to claim that large firms affiliated with the chaebols led Korea's industrialization.
7. See Jwa (2002b) where I address the critical issue of the effectiveness of regulating economic concentration. In general, policy to alleviate economic concentration by regulating large corporations rather than promoting competition will incur a substantial loss to the economy because it can destroy the incentives for large corporations to expand and this

completely ignores the intrinsic economic dependencies—specifically, regulating large corporations tends to decrease economic demand for SME products.

8. For example, the value of the won rose against the US dollar by 18% in 1988 alone. At the same time, new low cost competitors, notably China, appeared to challenge Korea's traditional roles in several sectors, which, together with the volatility in the world electronics market, led to balance of payments problems. Also wage increases far exceeded the gains in productivity.
9. Also, excessive private spending and real estate speculation were induced by the sudden increase in disposable income. As with Japan throughout the 1980s, the real estate market in Korea, which was also fueled by the government's policy to build two million houses in the new satellite cities near Seoul (especially Bundang and Ilsan) created a notorious bubble, which gradually, together with the increase in real wage, brought inflation to around 10% at the turn of the decade.
10. The KFTC initially dormant became increasingly active from 1987 onwards following Korea's transition to democracy.
11. See Jwa (2002b) for more details.
12. The real name system was the government's effort to mitigate corruption under the old system in which it had been possible to open accounts and conduct business transactions under false names, directly and indirectly fostering institutionalized corruption and illegal financial dealings. Also interesting to note is that during his 5 years in office, Kim Young-Sam removed and named six prime ministers, seven deputy prime ministers, four economic secretaries and 125 ministers.
13. Widespread deregulation actually began under the Roh Tae-woo administration in 1988. Soon afterwards, deregulation became a vogue in Korea whose objectives became somewhat confused. Kim Young-Sam adopted deregulation as one of the most important economic reform measures without resolving the misconception and confusion around the policy objective of deregulation. Often, deregulation in one area would be accompanied or followed by regulation in another, and furthermore, the path to liberalization or opening up of financial market and industry has been rigidly regulated—I have, for example, used the term "regulated deregulation" to characterize such inconsistency in Korea's deregulation efforts.
14. See Jwa (2001).
15. Furthermore, overvaluation may have been maintained to deliberately put large corporations "on their toes"—there was widespread perception among government officials that the chaebol had become complacent and there was need to exert pressure to make corporations work even

harder and to lift export performance. The government seemed to be following the example of how Japan tried to increase its competitiveness in the midst of the rising yen in the 1980s.

16. Liberalization of short-term capital and the increased frequency in negotiating for the rollover of short-term debt (often allocated for speculation purposes) increased the possibility of default. Jwa and Huh (1998, pp. 5–33), show how rollovers fell from about 80% in October 1997 to 50% in November to about 30% in December.
17. See Jwa (2001) for more details on the causes of Korean financial crisis from the same perspective.
18. An immediate effect of the crisis was the depreciation of the won to the US dollar—at the end of September 1997, one US dollar bought 915 won, but by year-end, the won had fallen to a record low of 1965 won.
19. See Jwa (2001) for more details on this.
20. See Jwa (2001, Appendix 8.2)
21. See Jwa (2001) for more details.
22. "Reform fatigue" is the syndrome or side-effect of too rapid and excessive reform, whereby the corporate sector, the labor markets, the legal system, and so on, are brought to a standstill due to exhaustion from too much reform.
23. "Management democracy" (or more precisely, the participation of workers in management decision-making) can disrupt a firm's intrinsic hierarchical structure. That is, the firm's command and control structure, the main coordination mechanism that allows the firm to be even more efficient than the market can be distorted if democratic or horizontal structures replace the hierarchical nature of firms. See Jwa (2002a).
24. The presumption that labor was underpaid during the industrialization because the authoritarian government suppressed union activities has been common understanding but is not empirically supported. Rather wage increases have been found to have never lagged behind labor productivity during the developmental era. See Park (2006).
25. We will return to this argument again later in Chap. 7.
26. This argument is from Alchian and Allen (1977) and Demsetz (1974).
27. In this regard, it is interesting to observe that social empowerment policies adopted in most developing as well as developed economies have increasingly turned into egalitarian policies, thereby losing their power to create incentives for growth and many economies have become financially unsustainable as well. This situation can also be reversed by infusing the economic discrimination incentive structure into the social policy. For more on this see the Chap. 7.

References

Acemoglu, Daron, and James A. Robinson. 2012. *Why Nations Fail: The Origins of Power, Prosperity, and Poverty*. New York: Crown Publishers.

Alchian, Armen A., and William R. Allen. 1977. *Exchange and Production: Competition, Coordination, and Control*, 2nd ed. Belmont, CA: Wadsworth Publishing Company Inc.

Bishop, Isabella Bird. 1970 [1897]. *Korea and Her Neighbors*. Seoul: Yeonsei University Press.

Demsetz, Harold. 1974. Two Systems of Belief About Monopoly. In *Industrial Concentration: The New Learning*, ed. H. Goldschmid, H.M. Mann, and J.F. Weston, 164–184. Boston: Little, Brown & Company.

Jwa, Sung-Hee. 2001. *A New Paradigm for Korea's Economic Development: From Government Control to Market Economy*. London: Palgrave.

Jwa, Sung-Hee. 2002a. Why Firms and Markets in Economics. *Seoul Journal of Economics* 15 (2): 277–294.

Jwa, Sung-Hee. 2002b. *The Evolution of Large Corporations in Korea: A New Institutional Economics Perspective of the Chaebol*. Cheltenham: Edward Elgar.

Jwa, Sung-Hee, and Chan-Guk Huh. 1998. Korea's 1997 Currency Crisis: Causes and Implications. *Korea Journal* 38 (2): 5–33.

Park, Ki Seong. 2006. Industrial Relations and Economic Growth in Korea. *Pacific Economic Review* 12 (5): 711–723.

CHAPTER 7

Eight Key Lessons from Korea's Development Experiences

Abstract This chapter comprises of 8 critical questions and answers that are meant to expose 8 key lessons from Korea's development experiences for developing as well as developed countries. These include the importance of development-friendly leadership, export-led growth and HCI drive by economic discrimination, corporate-growth led economic development (including empirical evidence), and the Saemaul Undong, as well as the slowdown due to economic egalitarianism that tends to diminish economic discrimination. Also emphasized is Korea's shared and polarized growth experiences. The chapter also looks at how development-unfriendly informal institutions can be transformed into development-friendly ones.

Keywords Development-friendly ED leadership · Economization of politics · Export-led Growth · Heavy and Chemical Industry (HCI) drive · Corporate-growth-led development · Saemaul Undong Shared and polarized growth · Transformation of informal institutions

S.-H. Jwa, *The Rise and Fall of Korea's Economic Development*,
DOI 10.1007/978-3-319-58065-4_7

Development-Friendly ED-Leadership of Park Chung Hee

Question 1: Arguably it has been widely recognized that the single most important critical factor in Korea's economic development success in 1960s–1970s was the leadership of Park Chung Hee. However, so far his leadership has not been fully analyzed in a way that could be useful to other national leaders or peoples. What are the features that distinguish Park Chung Hee's leadership? Here, I will try to characterize his leadership particularly from the perspective of economic development.

Pragmatic Leadership

Park's leadership can best be characterized by pragmatism. For example, he made the bold and pragmatic decision to set free and engage the services of eleven "corrupted" business leaders who were sent to prison as tax evaders following the military coup. Under the condition of paying back the taxes evaded and promise of participating in and contributing to the nation's economic development, Park decided not to confiscate their assets and corporations. This is a critical decision as he recognized that these business leaders, although condemned by somewhat political accusations reflecting populist sentiment of the public at the time, were the only people who knew how to manage a corporation and realized that he needed to utilize them to fulfill the fourth manifesto of the coup—to develop the economy. This decision took priority over the third manifesto, which was to clean up corruption, thus seriously risking the political justification for the coup.[1] Seen from the perspective of the new institutional economics, the fact that most of the leading businesses were subject to accusations of similar misbehavior implies that Korea's business environment at the time in general induced such behavior; for instance, such issues as tax evasion were not idiosyncratic behaviors but stemmed from institutionally distorted incentive problems that were endemic to the business sector as a whole. Therefore, the solution should be sought to reform the institutions rather than to selectively punish individual businessmen. In this regard, Park's bold and pragmatic decision turns out to be development-friendly in hindsight.

Later on, in order to acquire the necessary investment capital for development, Park made deals with Japan, Korea's former colonizer, which ultimately resulted in resuming diplomatic relationship. Park did so against intense opposition and nationwide protests, again taking a serious political risk. He dispatched the Korean military force to defend South Vietnam against communist aggression, again amid intense domestic political protests, only later proving this decision was a big bonanza for Korea's economic development. Park turned out to have made the necessary sacrifices on the western style democracy and sometimes human rights as he thought it necessary for the purposes of economic development. He often emphasized Korean way of democracy for economic development by arguing that the Western clothes do not always fit Koreans, or that "one size doesn't fit all".

Leadership Economizing Politics

Park understood very well that democracy in general is hard to blossom before economic development and particularly that modern western democracy emphasizing economic equality as well as the egalitarian socialist ideology could be very damaging to the economic development,[2] as declared by his number-one manifesto of the coup, "strengthening anti-communist stance". It so turns out that Park did not allow political considerations to override and contaminate his economic decisions. This is a very important point that demonstrates how he had always exercised economic discrimination in economic policy and strategy. Park did not permit political populism to influence his economic policy decisions, and was comfortable with placing economic bureaucracy above the political machinery when it came to economic decisions. In fact, where necessary he was always ready to utilize politics for economic development. He did so by even leaning to a rather authoritarian regime, in spite of severe criticisms by domestic opponents as well as foreign allies. In this context, the Saemaul Undong is a good educational example whereby political decision was kept away from distorting the economic discrimination principle, which will be further discussed in the later section. Furthermore, even the politically notorious *Yushin* or Restoration, through which he turned the political regime into an even stronger authoritarian one, can be reinterpreted as a vivid example of his efforts to keep the political sector from becoming a stumbling block in the achievement of the nation's long-term economic goals as well as national security. The promotion of defense industry, and in particular, building the Heavy and Chemical industrial base needed desperately by Korea at the time would otherwise have taken a much time longer than just a decade. It can be argued in this regard that he had always economized Korean politics for the sake of national economic development, and so his leadership can be characterized as one that "economized" politics, or one that put economics above politics.

Economically Discriminatory (ED) and Motivational Leadership

Park's key ideology was "*Shin-Sang-Pil-bul*" (신상필벌 in Korean or 信賞必罰 in Chinese meaning "Never fail to reward a merit and never let a fault go unpunished"), or "God helps those who help themselves", both meaning "dispensation of justice". This is as I have explained the key function of the market as well. As seen in so many cases of economic discrimination policies, Park was always ready to take this ideology and to push it even further. He can often be heard teaching his people about "*Shin-Sang-Pil-bul*" and hence he was a true teacher of ED—a teacher and establisher of the market. His leadership was truly economically discriminatory and motivational, i.e. development-friendly.[3]

Park was prepared to exercise economic discrimination even to the veterans and their families. He once said, "Relief recipients must conceive of self-reliance and self-help spirit, and try to become independent, appreciating the support given by the government. If they become self-complacent by counting on the government, then becoming independent is a long way to go. And we need to stimulate and motivate them by rewarding more support to those who have been successful. Otherwise relief recipients would be trapped under moral hazard. Because they would think that a certain amount of support will automatically be given by the government to them every year, they would not try to exert themselves to live better."[4]

Success Factors of High Export Performance

Question 2: How did Korea achieve such an extraordinarily high export growth? Korea's export-led growth strategy was a kind of public good adopted by many other developing economies in the 1960s and 1970s. There is no shortage of textbooks in international economics that are filled with export promotion strategies such as exchange rate policies, financial supportive policies, marketing strategies, regional integration such as FTAs, and oversea investment strategies. However, if one thinks about how many developing economies did in fact achieve such remarkable export growth as Korea did in the past 50 some years, the answer is not that many. What then was the reason for Korea's incredible export performances?

Export promotion policy had always favored the high export performers. As such, the policy was in fact a commitment by the government to support the better exporters for their hard work in earning more foreign exchange (dollars). Competitive rivalry to become the best performer prevailed for at least two decades and became thus a kind of cultural DNA of Korean firms. The provision of a sound macroeconomic environment such as stable domestic price level, stable and competitive but not overvalued exchange rate, and a system of export credit were of course important factors for export activities. But the Korean experience seems to show that such textbook recommendations are hardly enough. Together with and beyond that, government-led discriminatory policy support for high export performers is a necessary condition for the realization of extraordinary export performances.

A regular monthly meeting of the extended export promotion committee consisting of export-related ministers, export business representatives, commercial bankers and representatives of business associations led by President Park had been held since 1965. The meetings monitored the trends of monthly, merchandise-wise and regional export performances, and helped determine the policy direction for export promotion and for break-through of export bottlenecks.[5] At the end of every November since 1965 (commemorating the achievement of 100 million dollar export on November 30, 1964), the "National Export-day Ceremony" was held by the export promotion committee to select the best export performers, confer national achievements medals onto them and make them national heroes. On the day of the national export-day ceremony, all Korean exporting firms were subject to performance evaluation and ranking, and national recognition was bestowed upon successful exporters in a highly publicized medals ceremony, a citation that provided entrepreneurs with enormous social prestige. In this manner, all firms in Korea participated in the "export-beauty contest" and bankers were put in line ready to lend to the winners. This event was a kind of loan screening process by which high performing firms that passed the contest were provided export credit by the banks as well as honor and respect by the people. The contest did not end as a one-time event. Every year, on the same day of November, the ceremony was held in the same fashion for 15 years during Park's regime. The contest was open to each and every firm regardless of industry and size. This was exactly the kind of positive and beneficial government-led discrimination and motivation mechanism behind the Korean development experience. To Korean firms and entrepreneurs, exporting was likened to a life or death problem. If a firm was selected as a high performer in this contest, it would be provided with resources that would almost ensure its chance of future success; more bank credit and government subsidies and favors, and even more importantly perhaps, the opportunity for the owner CEOs to become national heroes. The only sure way towards business success in Korea was to become the high ranker in this export contest.

Furthermore, many of Korea's brightest young people started to dream of becoming successful exporters and national heroes. Also through this process, many innovative ideas in the export business were created and adopted over all areas of business. The end result is of course the booming export sector for Korea. Coupled with the "can-do spirit" embodied into Korean businessmen, Korea's business DNA was formed with the export promotion strategy.

What is important to realize is that the government through such "export contests" had placed economic discrimination policies at the center of economic growth. Also worth noting is that by placing a broad target that transcends the confines of any particular sector of the economy and by applying and repeating the same game every year, the "export contests" could not but diminish potential rent-seeking behavior of protected and monopolistic firms.

So what are some of the important lessons for export promotion policy from the Korean experience? The first is that it may be necessary to supplement the market's discrimination function by government-led discriminatory export promotion policy, which goes beyond the textbook case of export policies, especially if visible outcome of export growth is required and urgent. Government support that is differentiated and based on export performance is a key factor behind Korea's success.

In this context, a memoir of a government official who was then in charge of export promotion at the time is exceedingly illuminating. According to Won-Cheol Oh, there were four principles that the export promotion policy must follow[6]: "Firstly, do not help every business loosely. Promote only a few export items which are beneficial to our country's export specialization but one by one, not every item altogether. Secondly, not every selected company will be given support equally even though they produce selected priority items. Rather, support will depend on their export performances; those showing higher performance will be given more support. We must help those companies that follow us and exclude those that do not follow us. We should select the company, not the business area, for support. And the government should increase the number of supported companies gradually, and not consider them all for support at once. Thirdly, as long as those selected companies are successful at exporting, we should support them as much as possible. The examples including helping replace old machinery with the latest one and supporting those companies financially with either dollar or won, with coordinated support between the government and private sector, exempting tariffs on importation of capital goods and raw materials for export, lowering interest rates, providing a sufficient amount of operation money and free education for technical improvement, and permitting a business learning trip abroad (which was at the time very costly and rare). Lastly, the government will give a citation and a medal of honor to praise those companies' export achievements." These principles are perfectly in accordance with our discrimination and motivation strategy for industrial development.

The second lesson is that the selection of high performing exporters should be based on market performances through a transparent evaluation criterion so as to avoid any politically motivated intervention in picking the winners ahead of market signals.

The third is that this strategy should be open to all firms in all sectors and of all sizes and should be repeated consistently and regularly, thereby helping to promote keen competition among firms and minimizing the possibility of rent-seeking behavior in the business sector.

And finally, the export drive with such built-in performance-based incentive system will have a much better chance of success.

Success Factors of Industrial Policy: HCI Promotion Policy

Question 3: What are the Success factors of Korea's Industrial Policy (IP)? Was it ever successful? The truth is in the pudding; Korea's industrial policy under Park Chung Hee must have been successful because those promoted firms and industries are now the nation's leading industries and corporations. However, there remains not only skepticism among neoclassical economists who readily discredited industrial policy as inappropriate since it only distorts market allocation, but it is also true that there are very scant episodes of successful industrial policy in the 20th century worth noticing. Furthermore, Korea's industrial policy, particularly her HCI (heavy and chemical industry) drive, was officially declared as a failure in the 1980s by the Korean government and academics as well as the international community including the World Bank (1993). That may be the case, but today Korea's HCI drive has turned out to become the basis for Korean industrial dynamism and is now leading Korea's exports. How can we resolve this puzzle and what should we learn from this experience?

Debates on the Role of Industrial Policy in Korean Development

Let us provide a few competing explanations for Korean experience with industrial policy.

Explanation 1: (*Market fundamentalist type 1*)—Park worked extremely hard to establish Korea's industrial policy but there was not much impact on the economy. Then it follows that there is not much more to debate on industrial policy because Park did in fact follow the market principle and promote economic freedom in the market unwittingly, which is where the credit should go, in spite of the industrial policy in place at the time.[7] Market fundamentalists are firmly behind the market principle and economic freedom for economic development and therefore support the improvement of economic freedom if development is to be possible. This hypothesis recognizes Park's unintended contribution but not the industrial policy's contribution to the Korean economy. But what is not clear is what exactly it is about markets that make development possible and what is in fact meant by the market principle?

Explanation 2: (*Market fundamentalist type 2*)—Park did enormous harm to the Korea's growth by adopting industrial policy because industrial policy must cause resource misallocation by definition. Without Park's industrial policies, Korea would have performed much better with higher growth rates than about 10% per annum growth that had been experienced for 18 years under park's regime at the time.[8] This explanation recognizes neither Park's nor industrial policy's contribution to the Korean economy. This is a counterfactual historical argument which is rather difficult to verify.

Explanation 3: (*Naïve tautologist*)—Park's industrial policy is looked upon favorably and is acknowledged to have contributed to Korean economic success because his rule did in fact see Korea achieving an economic miracle. However no further explanation is provided as to exactly what is meant by successful or failed industrial policies. The conditions for successful industrial policy are not systematically investigated.[9]

Explanation 4: (*Strong industrial policy proponents*)—Park indeed succeeded because he intervened against the market.[10] Korea's industrial policy worked in the opposite direction to market signals when it came to resource allocation because Korea's HCI drive at the time was an attempt to move the industrial sector beyond labor intensive industries which had reflected the nation's relative comparative advantage. But no explanations are provided about why most of many developing countries adopting such industrial policy have in fact failed to meet expectations.

Explanation 5: (*Performance based ED*)—Industrial policy can be successful only if it can re-enforce the market's real function, 'economic discrimination'. Here, the market is viewed as a discriminating device which selects and supports the better performers and thereby matches rewards with performances as has been discussed in Chap. 4 above. What is important to realize is that successful industrial policy should support market-chosen survivors. Why? Markets are imperfect in the real world due to positive transaction costs and hence market-chosen best performers will not be fully rewarded for innovative efforts while this in fact creates positive external effects as others free-ride on the innovation.[11] This type of market failure is internalized mostly by modern corporations, but there is also a space for the government to re-enforce the market's discriminatory function by supporting the best performers. This could be particularly important not only during the developing country's catch-up period when weak market power needs to be supplemented by the government but also whenever the economy (developing and developed countries alike) gets trapped under long term growth stagnation thereby necessitating revitalization and redevelopment. The active role of organizations like corporations and the government in the developmental process is emphasized beyond simple market forces. Hence, we provide a new interpretation of industrial policy as a market reinforcing and promoting mechanism. This is the position taken in this study.

The validity of alternative explanations will depend on their relative explanatory power not only with regards to the extraordinary high growth trend of the developmental era (Korea in 1960s–1980s) but also for the continued declining growth trend in the post-developmental era of the past 30 years or so. Our explanation 5 contributes to a better understanding of the role of industrial policy by being able to consistently explain the whole 60 years' period of Korean development as done above, beyond the existing alternative theories which are unable to do so. We argue that industrial policy is a market-discrimination-function re-enforcing institution.

Theory of Comparative Advantage and Industrial Policy for Economic Development

The textbook theory of comparative advantage is not consistent with the concept of economic development involving the economic order transformation adopted by this book since this theory does not recommend deviation from existing industrial structure implied by existing comparative advantage that is dictated by given resource endowment. The agrarian economy is necessarily advised to stay as an agrarian economy as long as its resource endowment remains unchanged. This theory has become the basis for market-centric view of allocation economics which seeks efficient resource allocation given the fixed order or structure of the economy. Furthermore, it has worked as a powerful counter-argument against industrial policy designed to change the order of economy. In this regard, this theory has been criticized as a static theory and is not applicable to explaining the process of economic development. While the well-known theory of dynamic comparative advantage concurs with the need for industrial policy to transform the existing order of the economy, it still fails to overcome the criticism or weakness of industrial policy in general as will be seen below.

Seen from the new perspective of economic development, industrial policy as a means of changing the economic order or structure becomes a necessary instrument for economic development. Industrial policy has so far been under-appreciated in spite of its widespread uses probably because the pro-industrial camp has failed to provide a convincing theory of successful industrial policy just beyond ad hoc argument for its necessity. Moreover, there exist only very few examples of success in the modern era. I hope the discussions will clarify the success factors of industrial policy in the specific case of Korea as well as provide a theory of successful industrial policy in general.

Further Debates on the Pros and Cons for Industrial Policy and Implications

On the issue of industrial policy, several controversies remain. The most important first question is, "Who should choose the "winner"—the market or the government?" Proponents for the market argue that the market is more efficient in processing information; it knows better than the government and therefore should be allowed to pick the winner. This sounds reasonable. According to the argument of this study, however, the market is always executing industrial policy every day in the market, but a market alone-led developmental process remains destined to disappoint because of the inherent failure of market's discrimination function in the real world with positive transaction costs. In this situation, organizations such as the government or corporations are instrumental if transaction costs are to be suppressed because these institutions can supplement the weaker markets by re-enforcing or amplifying its discrimination function. We therefore provide a positive role for government industrial policy: The government can contribute to economic development not by intervening against market outcomes but by re-enforcing the market's discrimination function, i.e., market outcome. The implication is that government industrial policy should re-enforce the winners selected by the market if it is to be successful and sustainable. This is what we have referred to as government-led discrimination. In this context, the market and the government both jointly collaborate in picking and supporting the market winners after (ex post) but not before (ex ante) competition takes place in the market. We have mentioned this to be one of the thorniest issues of industrial policy, i.e. the idea of "picking the winner". Here, the concept of nudge may be relevant, where the government can help the market winner who is still somewhat weak.[12]

Secondly, as we have pointed out, how to pick winners before the market seems to have been the weakest point of industrial policy proponent so far. How do we know the winners before market competition works out in picking the winner? Industrial policy proponent like Dani Rodrik (2011) put aside this issue by arguing that the government should pick the *losers* instead of the winners. However, this seems somewhat contradictory, because if one can know the losers in advance, then one should know the winners too, since losers and winners are but different sides of the same coin. Here, the critical point to be kept in mind is that the market always performs industrial policy based on market outcomes, though imperfect as already argued above. And the best strategy for successful industrial policy therefore is the government-led economic discrimination based on market performances and results ex-post, rather than ex-ante. This is an important lesson learnt from Korea's experience with industrial policy.

Thirdly, from the first controversy discussed above, another key question is, "What should be the object to be supported by industrial policy? Is it Industry, functions, or corporations?" According to traditional industrial policy arguments, it is obvious that industrial policy should support the (infant) industry. However, mainstream neoclassical economists disagree: Support for specific industry, they argue, goes against the market mechanism and tends to distort market outcomes. Instead, the government should support the general functions of the economy such as R&D and education, and avoid directly targeting individual industries or firms. This has become somewhat the general rule of international trade, and any industry or firm-specific support has been declared as an unfair trade practice.

Let us make a few counterarguments to the neo-classical thought described above. First, industry and function are both not objects that would respond to incentives provided by government. Industry as well as economic function is indeed not subjective entities that pursue economic gains.[13] Rather, it is the corporation that pursues economic gain and is the subjective organism responsive to incentives. Second, if industrial policy targets the industry following the traditionalist or the functions following mainstream economics, such industrial policy cannot exercise economic discrimination because (1) the egalitarian populism widespread in the modern democracy favoring a 1/n support scheme becomes the dominant order of the day, and (2) focusing on industry or functions does not have a mechanism of identifying superior market-performing corporations. An egalitarian support system will be unavoidable, resulting in policy failure. Third, the ideal of a "fair, level playing field" in the international trade arena is in reality impossible unless the economic powers of individual nations are equalized and the level of and the support for general functions is equalized as well. In this regard, it may be argued that the global market is always an uneven playing field and, even worse, has actually been distorted by the global economic powers.

The main implication is that industrial policy should be perhaps renamed as a "corporation-promotion policy" that targets specific corporations and should be discriminatory in its support based on market performance.[14] Furthermore, the international rules of trade should allow room for developing economies to implement such a corporate promotion policy.

A fourth controversy is, "How should industrial policy be carried out?" A plausible answer to this nontrivial question seems now somewhat obvious. Industrial policy as a corporation-promotion policy should be exercised in a discriminatory manner based on corporations' market performances, by helping those corporations who help themselves, and this strategy should be regularly and consistently replayed through selection and re-selection or dropout as the case may be. Such policy cycle should be in regular intervals; e.g. monthly, biannual, annual, or every couple of years depending on the level of economic development, industry characteristics of production cycle, available resources, and political commitment. The objective is to help maximize the competition-promotion and motivational effects of industrial policy and at the same time minimize rent-seeking behavior on the part of corporation, which remains a potentially serious side-effect of traditional industrial policy.

Examples of Success and Failure of Korean Industrial Policy

Let us look at some examples of successful industrial policy in Korea. First, needless to say, the export industry promotion policy which is discussed in the previous section (Sect. 2 above) is the most conspicuous example of successful industrial policy based on the economic discrimination principle by supporting only the better and best export performers. Second, the HCI drive was launched in 1973 which permitted mainly internationally competitive, money-making companies to enter into the HCI sectors. Those chosen companies have benefitted immensely from government support, growing into successful global companies. HCI drive succeeded in spite of the official declaration of "failure" since these companies are today responsible for the development of major industries leading the Korean economy. The key success factor is the discriminatory industrial policy that allowed only the successful exporting companies in the global market to enter the HCI by imposing a strict capital adequacy condition requiring a 70 to 30 debt to equity ratio, and having most of the large sums of the initial investment requirement provided by the government with the company's own small seed money. Setting the capital and investment requirements this way acted as a kind of entry barrier to mediocre performing companies but was a big bonanza to competent exporters. There was, of course, active monitoring and restructuring process exercised when the government drove out insolvent companies. Here also we note that the government replicated and endorsed the discrimination function of the market.

Third, Korea's SME promotion policies in the developmental era was based on the economic discrimination as better performing SME were supported leading to their growth and expansion. SME promotion policies which started in mid-1960s were originally characterized as follows[15]: (1) Government cannot support every SME regardless of their performances and should be selective in its support. Noncompetitive SMEs should be allowed to go bankrupt and to be acquired by other competitive SMEs. (2) The SMEs is not differently treated from large corporations. (3) SMEs should specialize and be internationally competitive in its area of business. Even the Smaller Business Mediation Law in 1964, which is the origin of protecting special SME business area in Korea, incorporated this basic principle. However, this position has been given up in the post-1980s SME policies.

Fourth, the semi-conductor and IT industries promotion in 1980s permitted chaebols to enter even despite the strong chaebol regulation regime and anti-chaebol sentiments at the time. In the 1980s post-Park period, Korea's corporate policy had changed into a regime that regulated the expansion of large corporations. However, the 5th Republic right after the Park's regime had allowed those chaebols such as Samsung, Hyundai, LG, SK, KT, and Maxon to enter the semi-conductor and IT industries. This is diametrically opposite to the social, economic and political atmosphere at the time of regulating large corporations and supporting SMEs. Be that as it may, the policy was very discriminatory industrial policy.

Not all industrial policy in Korea were successful. Failed industrial policy in Korea are mostly characterized as cases of government-led anti-discriminatory industrial policy with egalitarian support. A notable example is the SME policy since the 1980s which gave up the previous economic discrimination mechanism replaced by the egalitarian "1/n" support system that turned out to be disappointing, and became a source of moral hazard and rent-seeking behavior on the part of many SMEs. Once government support loses the important feature of discrimination, it strips itself of the very incentives required for growth and motivation, thereby eroding the "self-help spirit" and resulting in inefficiencies. Another example of failure is the so-called venture industry promotion policy during the Kim Dae-jung government that lacked the economic discrimination features of successful industrial policy. It should now be unsurprising that it underperformed all expectations since it lacked the mechanism to discriminate high market performers over low performers. Here, the list of failures can be extended even further. They include the Roh Moo-hyun government's 10 future industries promotion policy and

Lee Myung-Bak government's green-growth industry promotion policy, which all under-performed compared to the expectation due to their egalitarian support system. It should be clear by now that a non-differentiated support policy is doomed to failure because it is void of any incentives for growth and expansion.

General Implications and Lessons for Successful Industrial Development Policies from Korea's Experiences

By way of summary and conclusion, we list in this section seven lessons for successful industrial policy based on Korea's experiences, consistent with the new theory of economic development.

First, government-led discriminatory economic policies are a necessary condition for success—support better performing corporations, period. Second, for the developmental incentive structure favoring high-performing agents to function smoothly, economic discrimination should also be built into the socio-economic system/framework. Third, it is vital to follow market signals and select the market-winners for support, rather than picking the "winners" *before* the market. Fourth, specific performance targets for selection should be clearly and transparently set. And this strategy should be regularly and consistently reenacted with the rigorous process of reevaluation of performances and reselection for support based on actual performance. Fifth, this policy strategy should be open to all firms in the economy. Sixth, the whole process of the policy strategy should be institutionalized into a formal rule. Such a rule should be fairly enforced. And finally, the general government's role of providing social infrastructure should also be strengthened and geared to meet policy objectives such as a strong financial support system, constant stream of skilled labor supply, R&D provision, and efficient supply of industrial parks.

Corporate-Growth-Led Economic Development

Question 4: How has Korea succeeded in developing corporations i.e. the chaebol to become a major player in the economy in such a short period? Arguably, economic development in the capitalist economy is a process of corporate growth. Korea's leading chaebols were in fact SMEs in the late-1950s and early-1960s but they have grown to world-class, internationally competitive corporation. How was this possible in just over a couple of decades?

Let's begin by making a few important observations. First, Samsung was a small shop exporting agricultural and fishery products that began in 1938. Samsung Electronics is now a global household name. Second, Hyundai started as a small auto repair shop. Hyundai Motors established in 1946 and Hyundai Construction established the following year have grown as part of the Hyundai Group family of corporations which includes Hyundai Motors, Hyundai Heavy Industries and the Hyundai Group. Third, the LG Group started as a small factory making facial cream and tooth paste in 1947 which has grown into LG Group Holding and another global brand, LG Electronics. Fourth, Daewoo was a small exporting venture which started only with 5 million won (approximately US$ 5000 at the time) in 1967 and grew into the Daewoo Group, and had a short span as the "most globalized" and best performing export company in Korea. The Daewoo Group was, however, dissolved in 1999 in the aftermath of the financial crisis but many of its member subsidiaries are still very much active in leading Korean industries under the same brand. Fifth, the SK Group started out as a small textile manufacturer in 1953 but has grown into the SK Telecom Group. Sixthly, POSCO (Pohang steel) started in 1968 from almost nothing to become one of the world largest and most competitive steel producing companies. Seventh, many other global Korean conglomerates started as small SMEs early when the new Republic was established in 1948.

Therefore, it is no exaggeration to state that corporate growth has led Korean economic development. Private organizations have played a critically important role in Korea's modernization and development. The role of the government (and other public organization) and the market in development remains an important controversial and unresolved issue in economic development theory and strategy, but there is little attention that goes to the role of private organizations (i.e. the corporation). One reason for this deficiency is because there seems to be no need for an organization like corporations in the perfectly competitive market models that have become the staple of mainstream economic theory. This is unfortunate because business corporations turn out to be the key critical player in the actual developmental process of the capitalist economy.

According to the new theory of economic development that we adopt, the growth process of business corporations from SMEs to major world class corporations is an important and almost natural process driving economic development. Corporate growth comes not only from internal growth but also from external growth. Therefore, having allowed active M&A activities in the corporate ecosystem will help speed up the growth of corporations. Furthermore, government-led industrial policy that supports the growing, better performing firms will help create an ecosystem favorable for high-performance firms by creating the right incentive and motivation for investment and expansion.

Korea's development experience is a vivid example of corporate growth-led development. Korea's industrial policy was a mechanism that helped speed up the growth of firms by activating, firstly, the internal growth path through helping those corporations who did better than others, and secondly, the external growth path through letting the failed and lesser performing firms to be acquired by better competitors. In fact, Korea's economic developmental strategy has turned out to be a corporate-growth strategy intentionally as well as unintentionally. We summarize this in four points: (1) Better performing exporters were given more financial support and tax benefits and were guided to merge and acquire the lesser performing exporters. (2) Only successful exporters that made money in the global market and accumulated enough capital were allowed to enter the HCI sector. (3) SME policy supported the better export performing firms with financial as well as tax benefits, and they were given a choice to merge with and acquire the poorer performing firms. In this continuous process of restructuring led by the government, the insolvent firms were always taken over by the solvent firms. (4) The end result of all export, HCI, and SME promotion policies taken together contributed in a synergistic way to help with the rapid growth of corporations. Seen from this perspective, one can argue that Korea's SME promotion policy was an essential feature of the Park Chung Hee era.

Finally we examined whether the data supports the corporate-growth-led development. It turns out that the behavior of Korea's aggregate income, GDP relatively closely mimics the pattern of the corporate assets variable in level and growth as shown in the Figs. 7.1 and 7.2. (All data are reported in Appendix 1) The correlation coefficient between per capita income and per capita corporate asset during 1968 to 2015 (all in nominal) turns out to be 0.926 and the one between their respective growth rates is 0.386, which all implies the pattern of corporate growth-led development.

Concerning the shared growth, one can check the correlation between Gini coefficient and corporate growth or GDP growth rates at the simplest level. For the period from 1990 to 2015 when the data

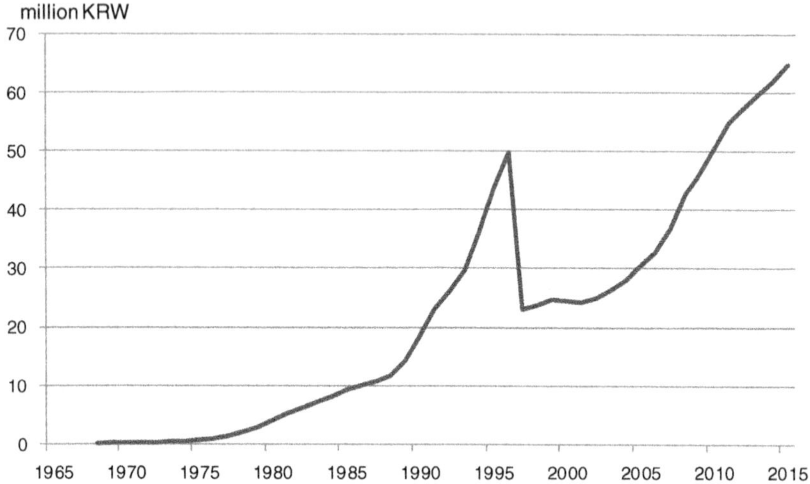

Fig. 7.1 Korea's per capita corporate assets. *Note* Korea's total corporate assets/total population. *Source* Author's calculation based on "corporate management analysis", the Bank of Korea

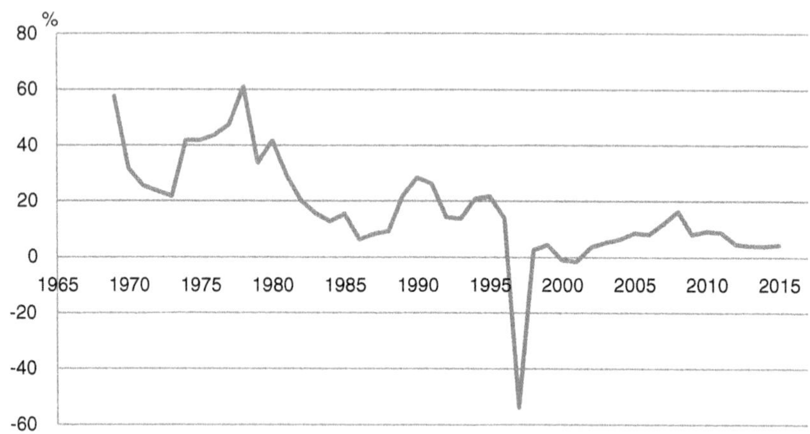

Fig. 7.2 Korea's per capita corporate assets growth. *Source* Same as in Fig. 7.1

on Gini are available, the correlation coefficient between Gini and corporate growth turns out to be −0.084 and the one between Gini and GDP growth, −0.762 implying a shared growth so that the growth of corporate asset as well as GDP accompanies the decline of Gini, an improvement of income distribution.[16]

With this data set, we conducted an empirical study to test the corporate-growth-led nature of the Korean economic development by adopting the corporate production function model presented in Chap. 4.[17] We have regressed per capita GDP on per capita total corporate assets with both in natural logarithmic scale. The results are as follows,

$$\begin{aligned} \text{Ln Y} &= \underset{(10.234)}{2.128} + \underset{(52.641)}{0.778}\,\text{Ln CA} + \underset{(4.523)}{0.014}(\text{Ln CA} \times D_1) + \underset{(15.066)}{0.064}(\text{Ln CA} \times D_2), \quad \ldots \quad (7.1) \\ &\text{Adjusted R - square} = 0.998 \end{aligned}$$

where, Ln Y is per capita GDP in natural log, Ln CA is per capita corporate assets in natural log, D_1 is the dummy variable which is equal to 1 for 1988–1996 (post-democratization to pre-financial crisis) and 0 for other years, and D_2 is the dummy variable which is equal to 1 for 1997–2015 (post-financial crisis) and 0 for other years. (Ln CA × D_1) and (Ln CA × D_2) intend to capture the variation of marginal productivity over time, respectively for 1988–1996 and for 1997–2015. The results are robust to heteroskedasticity and serial correlation. The t-values are in parenthesis and all coefficients are significant at the 99% level of confidence.

The results reported in the Eq. (7.1) can be interpreted as follows; first, on average for the whole sample, the marginal productivity of the corporate sector, the coefficient of Ln CA is estimated as 0.778 implying 1% increase of corporate assets brings roughly 0.778% increase of GDP.[18] Second, the marginal productivity turns out to have increased beyond 0.778 over time by 0.014% point for the period from 1988 to 1996 just before the financial crisis took place and by 0.064% point since 1997, respectively. While the marginal productivity has increased slightly over time as such, the growth rate of corporate sector (see Fig. 7.2) has significantly diminished especially since the financial crisis, thereby causing the trend of GDP growth rates to decline thereafter.

These findings imply the declining growth trend of Korea's GDP since the late 1980s (see Fig. 6.1 in Chap. 6) can be attributed to the very stagnant growth of the corporate sector in spite of the marginal contribution of the productivity improvement of corporations. The lost incentive to grow and expand on the part of corporations seems to be the main driving force to bring down the Korean economic growth.

This book has repeatedly argued that this is due to the growth-incentive lacking corporate policies, large corporate regulation to constraint their expansion and egalitarian SME support policy lacking the economic discrimination for the last 30 years since the late 1980s.[19]

Success Factors of Saemaul Undong

Question 5: What were the success factors for Korea's Saemaul Undong or New Village Movement? Was education/moral suasion enough to stimulate Saemaul Undong's "self-help spirit"? Was it government-forced? What other factors could possibly have played a role for success? Today, many developing countries looking for a model for rural development have turned to Korea's Saemaul Undong but apparently without much success; a real and proper understanding is seriously due.

President Park's ideology and policy of economic discrimination, "Reward good performance but penalize bad performance!", was the key success factor of the Saemaul Undong. Let us begin the story with a short background of the Saemaul Undong. Korea's farming and rural sector in general had been described as lazy and void of a "self-help spirit" and even hopeless for economic development by many observers in 1950s–1960s. Under Korea's historical tradition and path-dependence of the late-Chosun dynasty that did not allow much economic freedom nor provide any incentives to general public to seek economic affluence, such development-unfriendly behavior had long been established into Korean culture. All this of course hindered the prospect for economic prosperity. Circumstances needed to be changed. To make matters worse, the farming sector had lagged behind the urban-industrial sector after almost decade-long industrialization efforts in the 1960s. Against this background, Park Chung Hee decided to do address the situation, especially utilizing the then excess production of cement that was created by the demand slowdown in the East Asian market due to the first global oil shock in the early 1970s. The main purpose of the Saemaul Undong was to transform the peoples' development-unfriendly ideology to become development-friendly, by instilling the "self-help spirit" as well as to help improve productivity in the farming sector.

Central to the Saemaul Undong was the strategy of always supporting villages that helped themselves thereby igniting the "self-help spirit". The support which went to better performing villages succeeded in motivating other villages to actively participate in the Saemaul Undong and to work hard so as not to lag behind. Presidential statements by Park regarding the Saemaul Undong are particularly illuminating: "For those farmers who only dwell on one's own misfortune of being poor and complain that the government does not help them and that their poverty is due to others, it is impossible for them to overcome such difficulties even after hundreds of years. Supporting such people who are not self-motivated is a waste of money. Even a country cannot help those who do not help themselves."[20] This was the essential message repeatedly given by Park at the beginning as well as during the whole period of Saemaul Undong. He always went by the dictum, "Never fail to reward a merit and never let a fault go unpunished" and "God helps those who help themselves", or in other word, "dispensation of justice".

In the fall of 1970, the first year of the Movement, 34,000 villages in the whole country were identified and 200–300 sacks of cements together with a ton of steel bars were provided with the following message: do not distribute cements to individual households. They should be utilized for the villages SOC construction. The second message was: decide what projects are to be carried out from a lists of more than 10 potential projects for the movement recommended by the government and based on the consensus of village meetings.

Six months later, the government sent 50 professors affiliated with the government advisory committee and officials to evaluate performances of all villages using open as well as secret monitoring processes. 16,000 villages made some progress but 18,000 villages failed to do so with some not participating at all. With these results, heated debate followed as to how to proceed in the next round. The ministerial cabinet meeting decided to repeat the same support with more active focus on educating Saemaul Undong's "self-help spirit". But President Park overrode this decision in the midst of heavy objections by the ruling political party leaders. He declared rather that an economically discriminatory support system based on the first round performances should be pursued in which good performers are rewarded and bad performers are penalized. The government followed and decided that for 16,000 successful performers, more cement of up to 100–200 sacks would be additionally provided in addition to the amount provided in the previous year with a handsome amount of cash to some extraordinary top performers. For the 18,000 unsatisfactory performers, nothing would go to them and with a strong message, "You will not receive any government support from now on unless you show some progress at your own cost".[21]

In the second round, interestingly, 6000 villages out of those 18,000 villages did show some progress and, of course, the higher performing 16,000 villages continued to improve themselves as well. In the third round, the government picked the newly successful 6000 villages in the previous second-round for support together with continuously high-performing 16,000 villages.[22]

What Park did essentially was to classify villages according to their performances, the highest performing, self-sufficient ones as third grade, moderately performing, self-help ones as second grade and the lowest performing basic ones as first grade, and declared that the government would support always the third and second grade villages but leave out the first grade or nonperforming villages. Furthermore, the government favored the high-performing villages and sometimes left out the lesser performing ones when it came to other kinds of support such as water supply and electricity that were meant to help improve the infrastructure for the farming sector. What may be surprising is that such a strategy was totally opposite to the policy position adopted up by most governments after Park; it is common nowadays to find advocates arguing that government support should be directed to the first and lower grade villages, the basic or nonperforming people in general to remedy Korea's socio-economic situation.

It may make sense politically and socially perhaps to argue for the need to support and promote such villages that are behind. However, Park argued for the opposite. His remarks on the necessity for Saemaul Undong to be based on discriminatory principles are as follows: "As the result of supporting the 32,000 villages in the whole country to awaken farmers' and fishermen's strenuous spirit, though it wasn't that much, there were some villages which showed good performances while others didn't. With this experience, rejecting the idea of uniform support, we have decided to support only 16,000 successful villages, roughly half of the last year's number. It means that villages which did a poor job last year should stay back and will be left out of the project, and those which did well will be supported in the second year. This year's 16,000 villages will be examined in the fall for their performances and will be promoted to the upper third grade next year if they do a good job. And the flunked villages which got a bad score last year but, with greater efforts, become united and make progress this year, will be selected and be promoted to second grade with the same amount of aid in the next round. And then, if their scores are bad next year, they will be degraded but otherwise, they will be promoted to third grade. The promoted villages in the third grade if they do well will be upgraded to the fourth grade with full support. And this is the basic principle of governmental support for the Saemaul Undong. Why do we have to do it this way? The answer is simple. We have witnessed the results of uniformly helping all villages in the farming-fishing sectors which were not good as expected. I think we should help first those villages which are diligent and help themselves first. Even if those villages are neighbors with each other, it is always possible that some improve themselves in terms of their living standard while others fall far behind, depending on their efforts. It is rather unfair if we assist equally both villages, the ones that decide to degenerate through gambling, alcohol, and indolence and others are trying to better their lives. Those steadily self-improving villages will be able to stand on their own feet with a little more government support. Of course, others which are left behind would complain about it. The voices from villages which are lagged behind may sound louder than those from the well-behaving villages. But we should never mind those complaints."[23]

The success factor for Korea's Saemaul Undong is that the government had stuck to the economic discrimination principle (or "God helps those who help themselves") to support only the better performing villages and by doing so succeeded in motivating all villages to participate in the movement. In fact, the government created market competition for excellent performance and through this strategy was able to break the old path-dependent, development-unfriendly mindset. The government helped create a dynamic, competitive, development-friendly, "self-help spirit" as well as the "can-do spirit" among the people. The proposition, "Economic discrimination is a necessary condition for development" is vividly verified with Korea's Saemaul Undong.

Under the Saemaul Undong, and of course aided by the additional government efforts to improve income, the farming sector nationwide improved drastically in terms of household income and even surpassed the urban sector for a brief 5 years period after 1974. However, under the post-Park regime and thereafter of egalitarianism strongly influenced by the surge in political and economic democratization, Saemaul Undong changed into an egalitarian, "1/n" support system and economic discrimination was drastically weakened partly due to this change. Thereafter, the growth of farm sector income began to lag behind the urban sector and more importantly the farm sector restructuring continued to get bogged down up until now in spite of the fact that Korea has

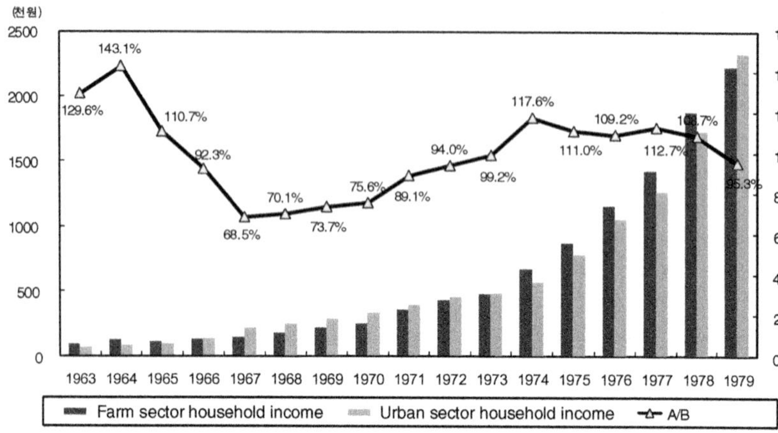

Fig. 7.3 Trend of farm (in *red*) and urban (in *blue*) sector average household income (Color figure online). *Source* The Bank of Korea

spent billions of dollars for that purpose over the last 30 years. And now the so-called Saemaul spirits or self-help, diligence and cooperation have unfortunately disappeared among the Korean people (Fig. 7.3).

Korea's Saemaul Undong has several important implications for development economics as well as for policy making: First, it provides important insights as to the importance of marketization of under-developed as well as stagnated economies. Many developing economies experience underdevelopment or stagnation even after having introduced the necessary market infrastructure such as private property right (PPR) and economic freedom, together with liberal democracy as a main political system. This had also been the case with Korea before Saemaul Undong was launched. Korea had spent almost 20 years building a full-fledged market system under a liberal democracy but without any real development. Here, the Saemaul Undong was an exemplar government-led economic discrimination strategy that created market competition and rivalry for success and thereby acting as the catalyst to awaken the sleeping instincts of the market-mind among the Korean people. With this strategy, the Korean farm sector began its transformation by joining the modern market economy. The government-led economic discrimination strategy as demonstrated with the Korean Saemaul Undong can therefore be described as a market competition-activating process that gives real impetus to the market system to really work for development and is arguably a necessary step for developing economies which have not been able to take the next step in really activating their markets. Furthermore, it is interesting to note that the strategy taken by Park, "Reward the good performers but penalize the bad ones", is exactly the combination of the two main incentive frameworks discovered recently by Behavioral Economics—"Gain framing and loss framing," which is perhaps the most effective incentive mechanisms to motivate people to change. The former refers to positive incentives towards desired behavior and the latter refers to taking back any given incentives from undesired behavior. It is interesting to see that the Saemaul Undong incorporated not only the gain framing idea by helping only those towns who performed better, but also the loss framing idea by taking back from the non-performing towns any government support which would naturally be expected to come again as their due share as it used to be by those villages still under the old non-self-help mind-set.[24] In this sense, Korea's Saemaul Undong was a precursor for Behavioral Economics and was implemented as a developmental policy on a nationwide scale.

Second, the Korean Saemaul Undong was in some sense a social reform program that "caught two birds with one stone". That is, it was successful not only in transforming the people's mindset (ideology) but also in increasing the productivity and income of the farm sector. In fact, the Saemaul Undong works effectively as a development policy as well as a social reform policy, both at the same time. The main success factor of course was the government-led economic discrimination policy. What needs emphasizing is that economic discrimination helped transform social policy into a development policy. The lessons learnt from this observation is that social policy that is intrinsically unsustainable because it consumes money without any direct and new creation of value-added is seen here to have transformed itself into sustainable policy as the distribution of social empowerment expenditures follow the economic discrimination principle and therefore act more like development policy in general. It is thus easy to see possible solutions to a failing, anti-discriminatory, egalitarian, incentive-non-differentiated social welfare system. Korea's Saemaul Undong experiences strongly imply that the adoption of economic discrimination in social empowerment policies can help rescue stagnated global economies burdened with increasing, nonproductive welfare programs.

Third, Saemaul Undong helps to reconfirm the success factors of industrial policy discussed in the sections above. In fact, Saemaul Undong exhibits a typical example of successful industrial policy, following precisely the same procedures for the successful industrial policy listed in the previous section.[25]

Reason for Korea's Economic Slow-Down: Economic Egalitarianism

Question 6: Why has Korea's growth potential declined for the past 30 years since the late-1980s?

In the post-developmental era, Korea adopted various new policy initiatives in the name of becoming a developed economy, including balanced social, economic, and regional development policies, and "economic democracy" that essentially seek economic equality. Although according to the World Bank standard, Korea has reached advanced nation status, Korea is presently experiencing many economic and social woes: a long declining potential growth trend, worsening shared growth with increasing income inequality and growth gaps across various sectors, low job creation for the youth as well as the old. There are also many other deteriorating social indicators such as low fertility rate, rapid aging population, and high education costs with collapsing public schools. Achieving a real developed economy status seems to be only a mirage for the Korean people at least in the foreseeable future. What has been the reason for such disappointing results?

During the post-political democratization era since the late-1980s, political concerns have overwhelmed economic concerns (we could refer to this as "politicizing the economy" with respect to the discussions above), which is in sharp contrast to the developmental era of the 1960s and 1970s. Basically Korea finds herself in the era of egalitarianism, development-unfriendly economic policies. For the past 30 years, Korea built and consolidated an egalitarian economic policy regime, dismantling the previous economic discrimination developmental policy regime set up by President Park. Examples of Korea's egalitarian policies adopted in the post-1980s period include: (1) special regulations on the expansion of large corporations and uniform non-differentiated SME support system; (2) adoption of balanced regional development policy strictly limiting new entry as well as the expansion of the existing production facilities of large corporations in the Seoul and Gyeonggi-do metropolitan area; (3) similarly restricting new entry of 4-year universities as well as student enrollment of existing universities in the Seoul and Gyeonggi-do metropolitan area; (4) establishing an education-equalization system sacrificing academic excellence; and (5) adoption and strengthening of the somewhat flawed European-style welfare system.[26]

Korea gradually in the early post-Park era and rapidly in the recent decades has embraced the European-style social democratic system. An interesting observation here is that Korea not only had replicated and free-ridden on successful Japanese knowhow during her developmental era, but also has followed the failing Japanese move to social democracy of the past 30 years.[27]

All in all, the egalitarian economic policy regime of present Korea is the primary cause for her economic slowdown. We need repeat here that according to the new developmental theory, egalitarianism is a sufficient condition for economic stagnation, because egalitarian economic policies by negating economic discrimination removes the incentives for economic agents to better themselves by treating all agents equally regardless of their effort and achievements. An extreme regime of egalitarianism will try to even things out in such a way that economically better-performing agents will be completely discouraged not to work hard (differentiate themselves) and the economically less successful agents will tend to become rent-seeker by sticking to the status quo falling further into moral hazard.

Hence, a policy regime that does not allow for economic differences and inequalities will by definition be development-unfriendly. Communism, socialism, social democracy, and populist democracy, which all pursue economic egalitarianism, are destined to disappoint when it comes to producing economic growth and development. Korea unfortunately has been moving towards such a regime of seeking economic equalities including equal regional development and social equality as has been mentioned above.

It should also be noted that the anti-discriminatory post-Park era is unable to deliver on the high expectation of Korea becoming an advanced developed nation. It looks like economic policy has been transformed and implemented as if it were social policy of the egalitarian redistribution type, i.e., "1/n" allocation among all economic agents.

Korea's Experiences of Shared and Polarized Growth

Question 7: How had Korea been able to achieve such a remarkable shared growth performance during the developmental era, whereas she has been experiencing a polarized growth since then?

Korea has been credited as an excellent model case for shared growth, as confirmed by the World Bank (1993). Korea achieved the fastest growth while maintaining remarkable equal income distribution at least until 1990 (see Fig. 7.4). How was Korea able to achieve a shared growth for growth-and-distribution, export-and-domestic sectors, large-and-SME sectors, as well as manufacturing-and-service sectors for the developmental era? Over the past 30 years or so, however, the nature of Korea's shared growth has been weakened. In particular, growth and distribution altogether has continued to worsen (see Fig. 7.5 and Fig. 6.1). What reasons are behind this reversed trend?

During the developmental era, Korea's exporting firms were given many kinds of support by the government under economic discrimination policies, and they were encouraged to reinvest their export revenues freely in the domestic market. The export boom was naturally translated into a domestic investment boom in the manufacturing sector by the growing export firms which in turn created a steady demand for the SME sector as well as for the services sector and enhanced domestic job creation. The chain reaction of this demand trickling-down can be credited for shared growth between export and domestic sectors, large export firms and the SME sectors, manufacturing and service sectors, and most importantly the ever improving income distribution accompanied by continuous job creation. This virtuous cycle was led by the government's export promotion and industrial policies based on economic discrimination.

However, as already mentioned, Korea chose to enter into an egalitarian economic policy regime, at first slowly during the first half of the 1980s and then rapidly since the late-1980s. Korea has adopted a systematic regulatory regime that directly intervenes in large corporations' investment activities, while having introduced a non-discriminatory, reverse-discriminating SME promotion policy framework. Furthermore, the anti-chaebol sentiment has grown further and has become a source of the anti-business regulation system propagated by populist democracy, for various concerns, whether right or wrong, disregarding the history of corporate growth during the developmental era. For example, not only the general public but also many economists seem to agree that the chaebol

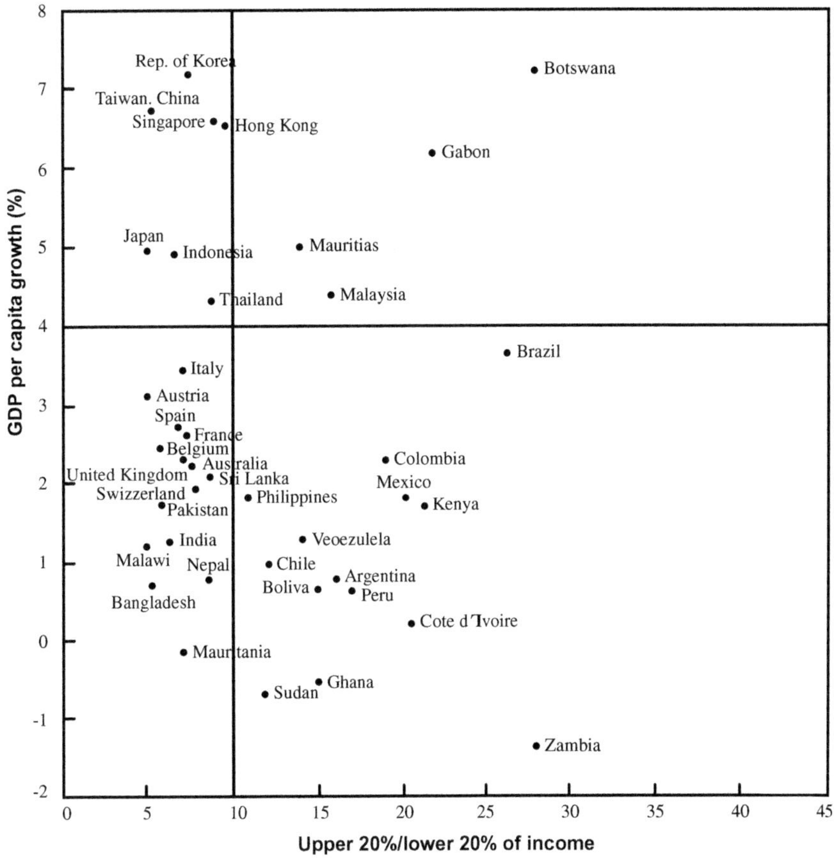

Fig. 7.4 Shared growth experiences (Avg. over 1965–1989). *Source* World Bank (1993, p. 31)

are a product of unfair government favor and that President Park adopted a pro-chaebol and anti-SME position. This book has argued that such beliefs are misguided.[28] Labor unions that have been encouraged to help the socially-weak have instead turned into militant labor organizations, and the wage hike has consistently surpassed labor productivity increase since the late-1980s. In addition, the Act for balanced regional development regulating the growth of Seoul and Gyeonggi-do metropolitan areas has placed strict prohibition on large corporations' business activities

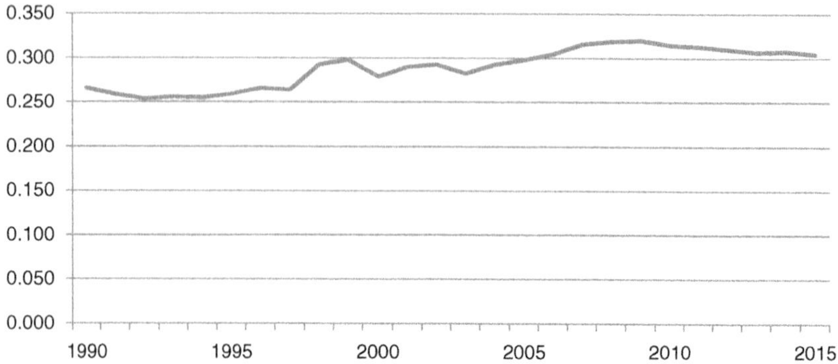

Fig. 7.5 Rising trend of Korea's Gini coefficient for Market Income. *Source* The Bank of Korea

from increasing the size of or newly building of plants and factory in the regions that actually have the best competitive advantages in the country. All these changes have driven large, most capable corporations to seek opportunities abroad in order to survive the ever increasing global competition. The export revenues of the large exporting corporations have either begun to seek foreign destinations for investment or simply remain in the vaults of large multinational banks. From then on, job creation slowed down and the virtuous cycle of various shared growth turned into a vicious cycle in which the domestic investment growth of the large corporate sector was halted with negative repercussion to the other sectors (See the data and figures on investment in Appendix 1.). The shared growth mechanism was eroded, and the so-called economic polarization encroached on the whole economy. With this egalitarian policy regime in place, which is development-unfriendly, Korea has shown a disturbing and ever-declining growth trend together with worsening income distribution.

The lesson is simply that we cannot afford to neglect the role of corporations and the importance of economic discrimination for economic growth and development. We should beware of the egalitarian trap.

Transforming Informal Institutions into Development-Friendly Ones

Question 8: Informal institutions influence the pace and fate of society's economic development by directly affecting peoples' economic behavior as well as by indirectly affecting formal institutions which in turn influence peoples' behavior. Therefore, it is critical for economic development to have development-friendly, i.e. economically discriminatory, informal institutions. During her developmental era, Korea was able to escape from the development-unfriendly informal institutions in the 1960s and 1970s, but since the 1980s she has reverting back to the old development-unfriendly informal institutions. What is the reason behind this trend?

Many Korean observers have argued that Korea's remarkable growth in the 1960s and 1970s derives much from the "can-do spirit" which is one of the most important development-friendly informal institutions. This is in stark contrast to the 1950s and before when Korea had been described as a "hopeless country" by many economic specialists and observers. So where did this "can-do spirit" originate and how has it been possible for ideology to have been so drastically transformed from a negative to a positive one? Arguably its source is Park Chung Hee economic discriminatory leadership by adopting economically discriminatory institutions and policies that was the critical factor for the creation of this can-do spirit.

As we have already discussed, the Korean mindset was historically development-unfriendly, dependent and unmotivated for economic progress. Korea under the late-Chosun Dynasty had not allowed, for example, a well-specified and protected property right system under which land ownership was allowed only to the King and the nobility. The traditional landscape was characterized by the economic as well as political systems under the control of a strong Confucian monarchy state, as well as the oriental social caste system of scholar-farmer-artisan-merchant. Furthermore, most farmers in particular had lived for long periods under the exploitive system laden with corrupt local public officials. Therefore, with hardly any economic incentive for hard work Koreans became rather passive and defensive. Under the condition of restricted social mobility across the social classes molded by the caste system, industrial and commercial activities led by the lowest classes had hardly any chance for development. Even amongst the higher classes of scholars, the only path to success involved reading and interpreting the Chinese liberal arts and philosophy and mastering the Chinese calligraphy for writing in order to pass the civil exams and become government officials. Needless to say such activities are unproductive from an economic standpoint. And the caste system did not just act as a constraint to people from engaging in science, industry, and commerce, but also life in such activities were considered downright shameful and disgraceful. After having lived under such conditions for more than 500 years, Korea's development-unfriendly way of thinking and economic behavior became somewhat fixed and permanent; it defined Korea's tradition and culture. Furthermore, the extractive Japanese rule for 36 years, although it exposed Korea to modern economic institutions, did little to change things and only reinforced the old tradition and culture.

Even after the establishment of Korea as a nation in 1948 and up until the early-1960s, many observers saw no hope for economic progress because they deemed Koreans as lazy and unmotivated for economic improvement given their historical tradition and culture. However, as we have explained above, it turns out that Korean people's way of thinking as well as their economic behavior was drastically transformed towards becoming a self-help and can-do society and development-friendly during the modernization era from the early-1960s. That notwithstanding, the situation seems to have reversed itself over the past 30 years or so. What were the driving factors behind these changes?

As a way of attempting an answer to this puzzle, it is worth reemphasizing that Korea's economic policy under Park's leadership was based on the economic discrimination principle. Such economic discrimination policy paradigm was the key factor that contributed to the transformation of Korea's historical tradition and culture during the developmental era. We have seen that with economic discrimination firmly placed at the heart of policy-making for almost two decades through the implementations of the export promotion policy, SME promotion policy, Heavy and Chemical Industry promotion policy, Saemaul Undong and all other social developmental polices, the Korean people successfully transformed themselves into a somewhat different kind of people believing in self-help and embracing the "can-do spirit".

Educational campaign and propaganda about the importance of self-help for one's economic improvement can be helpful in this transformation process but the key factor is the setup of development-friendly economic institutions and policies which create new "rules of the game" declaring, for example, that "if you behave in the self-help manner, then you will be given social recognition as well as monetary rewards accordingly or otherwise you will be given nothing and be left out". People tend to change their thinking and behavior willingly and permanently only when such change turns out beneficial to them and the underlying institutions remain effective for a sustained period of time. Breaking up the old mindset and behavioral habits requires the introduction and effective enforcement of new institutions with incentives properly aligned under the new rules.

In sum, Korean peoples' "can-do spirit" was made possible by putting in place the economic environment in which those people who helped themselves were treated favorably, and by maintaining this strategy consistently and stubbornly for a sustained period of time. This motivated people to work for economic progress. As we have seen, the government introduced highly discriminatory policies and institutions that effectively provided more chance and opportunity for success to those who helped themselves. The Korean people started to believe that the harder one worked, the higher the chances for success granted to them, and this is the essence of the "can-do spirit". Through this, people transformed themselves from hopeless to the hopeful citizens.

This however did not last. Korea's political environment turned out to be a critical constraint on the feasibility of continuously enforcing economic discrimination policies. It is now the case that the democratic political system in general, especially when turned into the populist democracy emphasizing economic egalitarianism[29] has worked against economic discrimination as has been experienced by Korea since the late-1980s. Once such democratic political regime based on the one-man-one-vote system was introduced and began to provide an easy political channel for the people without the "self-help spirit" to speak for their self-interest, the stage was set for an organized challenge against the economic discrimination policy regime under the plural party system, which made it difficult to maintain and enforce economic discrimination in the economic and political realms. This is because, under such a populist democracy, political equality is easily imposed upon the economic policy-making and implementation arena, translated as economic equality. This has been the case of Korea since the late-1980s when political democratization took place. Now more than ever, the Korean people's way of thinking and economic behavior have become more and more dependent in nature where many blame others for their economic misfortunes (just as they did in the old tradition and culture). At the same time, the economy has been suffering from long-term economic stagnation for more than two decades now. From this observation, one can see the importance of protecting economic discrimination in economic policy making from the influence of populist democracy that seeks economic equality, in order not to interrupt economic progress. Here again, the importance of economic discrimination political leadership cannot be over emphasized.

Notes

1. The manifestos of the military coup (revolution) led by Park Chung Hee on May 16, 1961 can be summarized as follows: 1. Re-enforce the anti-communist policy, 2. Respect international treaties with the free world allies including the UN, 3. Clean up social corruptions and reestablish the social morality, 4. Eradicate poverty and seek national prosperity, 5. Seek national unification by improving the power to win the communists, 6. Get back to the military duty after accomplishing these tasks. However, for economic development, Park Chung Hee made a pragmatic decision for the fourth manifesto over the third one early on after the revolution. According to a behind-the-scenes story, the Korean Economic Council, the former body of the Federation of Korean Industries (FKI) and businessmen like Dongwook Lee are known to have strenuously insisted on the abolition of the Anti-corruption Act, and it is also said that the then Chairman of Samsung group, Byungchul Lee also claimed the same. Chairman Lee at the time was staying in Japan but in fact was in hiding against his will so that he could avoid imprisoned, unlike the fate of other major business leaders. At that time, Chairman Lee had been pointed out for suspicion of unjust money-making from various wrongdoings such as tax evasion. After many twists and turns, Chairman Lee returned to Korea and upon his arrival at the airport was summoned to Park Chung Hee, the leader of the coup, to discuss the ideas for economic reconstruction. According to memoir of Chairman Lee (1986), while he suggested that it would be much better to set free those business leaders than to keep them in prison and to take advantage of their business knowledge, Park maintained to punish them because people would not accept their release. The business leaders, however, were released shortly after following Park's command.
2. See Jwa (2017) for the general exposition and logics of this proposition.
3. Broadly speaking, the leadership quality of Park Chung Hee turns out to be so outstanding, mostly being consistent with the nature of good leadership presented by Gardner (1993) and others. An interesting example of economic discrimination leadership in business sector can be found with Jack Welch, the former chairman of GE, while he uses the phrase, economic differentiation for economic discrimination. See Welch (2005).
4. Cho et al. (2003), p. 266.
5. Support policies at the time for exporting companies included: 1. 50% reduction of export income tax and corporate tax for export companies

earning foreign currencies, 2. Exemption of import duties on the raw materials for export production, 3. Special low interest offered to the export finance, 4. Establishment of KOTRA to collect information on the oversea export markets and to support export marketing and of Goryeo Trade under the Korea Trade Association to support SME export activities, 5. Promotion of export manufacturing companies, 6. Honor prizes awarded to the persons and companies who contributed to the nation's export promotion, based on the national law of the prize. See Kim (1990), p. 133.

6. I provide here my translations from Oh (1995, vol. I, p. 233). Oh was the then first Industrial Director of the Ministry of Commerce and Industry.
7. World Bank (1993).
8. See Sakong and Koh (2010), which is the general consensus around the Korean government think tank, the Korea Development Institute.
9. Chang (1994, 2002).
10. Amsden (1989).
11. For this point, see the previous discussion in the Chap. 4.
12. See Thaler and Sunstein (2008) for the usefulness of "nudge" in public policy.
13. Industry is an artifact created for the convenience of economic analysis, i.e., constructing a market supply curve to derive price parameter by assuming identical firms (or the representative firm) and aggregating them in perfectly competitive model, while all firms are different and standing their own as implied by Edward Chamberlin's theory of monopolistic competition and Joan Robinson's theory of imperfect competition. On the other hand, while the functions need to be improved for the efficiency of the market as well as the corporate firms in general, it is inevitable that the public policy should target superior agents, individuals, firms or organizations, capable of the needed functions under the economic discrimination principle. Therefore, from the perspective of public policy which tries to influence the behavior of agents by providing different incentives, the agents such as corporate firms, individuals or organizations could be more appropriate policy target rather than industry and function, while the latter ones have their own valuable uses in other contexts.
14. It turns out that Korea's export promotion policies were also company-focused. The principles of export promotion discussed in the previous section on the export promotion issue are all in accordance with our firm discrimination policy argument. Especially, the second principle for selecting an export company rather than an industry for support is an interesting example which shows the significance of the corporation-promotion policy over the traditional industrial policy in Korea.

15. Quoted from the memoir by Oh (1995, Vol. II, pp. 16–17), the then first Industrial Director of the Ministry of Commerce-Industry.
16. However, the correlation coefficients between Gini and the levels of corporate assets and GDP turn out to be 0.512 and 0.875 respectively, implying the shared growth hypothesis in the case of Korea holds only in the context of the growth of corporate assets as well as GDP rather than the level of corporate assets as well as GDP. The faster growth of corporate sector and GDP will help bring down the Gini. In the cross country context, however, Jwa (2017) reports the shared growth in the context of the level. It seems that the true nature of the sharedness of the corporate and GDP growth needs further empirical scrutiny. The difference could be due to data limitation, too short series of Gini as well as possible measurement errors in corporate asset used.
17. Refer to the section *Implications on Macroeconomic Growth and Productivity Analysis* in Chap. 4.
18. It is interesting to see Korea's corporate marginal productivity, 0.778 turns out to be double of the world average, 0.390 reported in Jwa (2017).
19. As explained in the note 13 in Chap. 4, the constant term in Eq. (7.1) can be interpreted as per capita income of the imaginary agrarian economy without corporate sector. The estimated constant term, 2.128 which is the natural log of the per capita income of the imaginary agrarian economy can be converted into about 8.4 Korean won (equal to roughly a little less than 1 cent in $), implying Korean old agrarian society had been living pennilessly under the absolutely starving level of income. On the other hand, it is interesting to see that per capita income of the imaginary agrarian economy of the world was estimated at $245 in the context of the cross country corporate production function estimation as shown in Jwa (2017).
20. Re-quoted from Kim (1997), p. 257.
21. As told by Jung-Ryum Kim, the then executive senior secretary to the president, the decision-making procedure of this discriminatory support was as follows: The cabinet council decision was to support equally in the second year as the first year, but the President insisted on discriminatory support. Then, Jun-Sik Gil, the then general secretary of the ruling Republican Party and Hyun-ok Kim, the then Minister of Domestic Affairs and later a group of the most influential politicians of the ruling party tried to persuade the President to adopt the equal support scheme by mentioning the potential political risks, but the president firmly stuck to his decision on discriminatory support. His firm principle was "Never fail to reward a merit or let a fault go unpunished."
22. The performance record of the Saemaul Undong in the text is from Kim (1990), pp. 189–190.

23. Re-quoted from Cho et al. (2003, p. 274). It seems that in this quotation that the total number of villages 32,000 should be read as 34,000 according to Kim (1997).
24. See Kahneman and Tversky (1979) and Gneezy and List (2013) for these incentive mechanisms.
25. Essentially the application of economic discrimination.
26. For more, see the list of Korea's egalitarian policies in Chap. 6 on evaluation of post-Park era.
27. See Jwa (2017) for how Japanese economy has been trapped in the egalitarian policy regime under social democracy since the mid-1970s ending up with the lost 2 decades.
28. See the discussions in Chap. 6 and this chapter on corporate-growth-led economic development above for this argument.
29. This type of political regime can also be called as egalitarian democracy or social democracy and the like emphasizing the economic egalitarianism under democracy as already discussed in previous Chaps. 4 and 5.

References

Amsden, Alice. 1989. *Asia's Next Giant: South Korea and Late Industrialization*. New York: Oxford University Press.

Chang, Ha-Joon. 1994. *The Political Economy of Industrial Policy*. New York: St. Martin's Press.

Chang, Ha-Joon. 2002. *Kicking away the Ladder: Development Strategy in Historical Perspective*. London: Anthem Press.

Cho, Gap-Jae, and Eun-Joong Kim. 2003. *YuiDaeHan CEO, Park Chunghee eui Teuk Myung* (In Korean). OulGan ChoSun: 242–277.

Gardner, John W. 1993. *On Leadership*. New York: The Free Press.

Gneezy, Uri, and John A. List. 2013. *The Why Axis*. New York: Public Affairs.

Jwa, Sung-Hee. 2017. *A General Theory of Economic Development: Towards A Capitalist Manifesto*. Cheltenham: Edward Elgar.

Kahneman, Daniel, and Amos Tversky. 1979. Prospect Theory: An Analysis of Decision Under Risk. *Econometrica* 47 (2): 263–291.

Kim, Jung-Ryum. 1990. *Hankook KyungJaeJungChaek 30 NyunSa* (In Korean). ChoongAng IlBoSa.

Kim, Jung-Ryum. 1997. *Ah, Park Chunghee, KimJungRyum JungChiHaeGoRok* (In Korean). ChoonAng M&B.

Lee, Byung-chul. 1986. *Hoam JaJun* (In Korean). ChoonAng IlBo.

Oh, Won-Cheol. 1995. *Hankook Hyung KyungJae GunSul* (In Korean), Jun 5 Guon, Kia KyungJaeYunKooSo.

Rodrik, Dani. 2011. "Perspectives on the New Industrial Policy" a PPT Presentation at the International Conference on Rethinking Industrial Policy

in the Era of Global Socio-Economic Restructuring, Organized by Korea Institute for Industrial Economics and Trade, in Seoul, December.
Sakong, Il, and Youngsun Koh (eds.). 2010. *The Korean Economy: Six Decades of Growth and Development, The Committee for the 60-years History of Korean Economy*. Seoul: Korea Development Institute.
Thaler, Richard, and Cass Sunstein. 2008. *Nudge: Improving Decisions About Health, Wealth, and Happiness*. Penguin Books.
Welch, Jack. 2005. *Winning*. New York: Harper Business.
World Bank. 1993. *The East Asian Miracle: Economic Growth and Public Policy*. New York: Oxford University Press.

CHAPTER 8

Reproducibility of the Korean Economic Miracle

Abstract This chapter considers the reproducibility of the Korean economic miracle in the modern era. The chapter begins by repudiating the myths of the Korean economy stated in Chap. 2, and then argues that indeed, albeit various difficulties and drastic change in the socio-political landscape, the replicability remains rather positive. What can be replicated is the infusion of the economic discrimination principle into the nation's institutions and policy-making led by strong leadership.

Keywords Repudiation of myths against Park Chung Hee paradigm
Replicable economic discrimination (ED) meme

This chapter considers the reproducibility of the Korean economic miracle. Here the question is, "To what extent can Park's leadership and policies be replicated in the twenty-first century?" That is, "To what extent can Korea's experience be benchmarked by late-comer developing and developed economies as well?" In order to answer this question, I will begin by dismantling the myths against the Korean Miracle presented at the outset of this book which are to a considerable extent shared among Korean scholars, politicians and intellectuals as well as the international circles of development theorists and practitioners.

S.-H. Jwa, *The Rise and Fall of Korea's Economic Development*,
DOI 10.1007/978-3-319-58065-4_8

Repudiation of the Myths Against the Korean Success

Myth one argues that President Park Chung Hee's economic policy paradigm during Korea's miracle years do not and should not hold any lessons for Korea in the later years as well as for other countries due to his non-democratic, authoritarian leadership and political regime. Now it is hoped that this myth is effectively repudiated by the arguments in this book. Park's relatively authoritarian political regime may be partly due to Korea's unique national security situation during the Cold War era and partly due to his firm belief, right or wrong, that true democracy can only blossom after or at least with the achievement of the priority goal of making Korea prosperous, a goal which was then thought to have been imperiled by an immature Western style democracy. In this regard, it is interesting to recollect that not a single economic policy and/or economic project received any kind of support or blessing by opposition political leaders or parties during his rule. Be that as it may, it turns out that his economic success can be attributed to his economic discrimination leadership and economic discrimination policy paradigm as discussed in Chap. 7, rather than to his authoritarian politics in any systematic way. Therefore, there is no grounds to argue that Park's success is a byproduct of his authoritarian politics and to claim that no lessons can be learned for twenty-first century democracy. Rather, more interesting lessons should be drawn from Korea's failed experience with anti-economic discriminatory egalitarian democracy over the last 30 years, namely that democracy without economic discrimination can be perilous to economic prosperity. In this regard, democratic leadership that embrace development-friendly ED-position could be a precondition for economic take-off of developing economies as well as economic revitalization of non-developing or stagnating developed economies.

Myth two argues that Park's economic policy regime adopted strong, government-led industrial policies by directly intervening in the market place and therefore, cannot be a successful benchmark for other economies. I think this myth is now effectively repudiated by industrial policy argument in Chap. 7, and it is now the time to fully understand the new insight on the successful industrial policy from Korea's experiences. Korean success should be seen as a hope for development seekers. In this regard, the general theory of economic development whose centerpiece is the holy trinity of economic development, market, corporation and government should be a theoretical guide to the successful role of the government in economic development.

Myth three sees Park's economic policy regime as having created concentration of economic power by promoting large corporations with pro-chaebol corporate policies, which largely worked against small-and-medium-sized enterprises (SME). Corporate-growth-led development argument in Chap. 7 provided a strong counter-argument: at its core, Korea's corporate-promotion policy was very much an SME promotion policy and in fact, turns out to be one of the best examples of successful SME promotion to be learnt by any development-seeking economies. Economic power concentration toward best or better performing corporations is natural process of development. While there will always be political incentives to directly regulate the expansion of those corporations, such policy runs the risk of killing the very incentive for corporations to grow, hurting growth and development. In this regard, it should be noted that any potential monopolistic implication of the ED-corporate promotion policy can be effectively handled without killing the incentive to grow by allowing more entries of potential as well as actual competitors.

Myth four is to argue Park's regime has created unbalanced regional, sectoral, and corporate development, being incompatible with balanced development. However, this is not only against the general theory of economic development that says economic development is by nature a lopsided affair but also against the historical fact that Korean growth during Park's regime was one of the best shared growth experiences in the world as discussed in the previous chapter. It is time to totally reorient the development economics paradigm from normative to positive economic thinking along with the ED-development principle.

Replicable Meme, ED-Principle for Successful Economic Management

Now with the barriers against the replicating of the meme of economic success erected by unfounded myths removed, I will discuss the reproducibility of Korea's success miracle story.

This book has tried to generalize the Korean experiences of the miracle years as replicable success-knowhow, (1) by sorting out the principle of successes and presenting a replicable blueprint for how to initiate and sustain the development process; one could say a kind of business plan for national economic management, rather than just description of what to do for development without providing an answer to how to go about it, and (2) by showing that the post-Miracle years' experiences which went against the success-knowhow of the miracle years also went against all hopes and expectations; a disappointing path that is not advisable for development-seeking economies, regardless of the level of development.

The key point to learn from Korea's success is the importance of economic discriminatory institutions and policies at all levels of the society's strata and in every corner of the society. While I understand the world political-economy order has changed and may not readily accept economic development based on economic discrimination, one nonetheless cannot expect economic development without economic discrimination policies in place.

No doubt it may be difficult today to replicate and reproduce Korea's past economic environment. The trade environment favorable to developing capitalist market economies during the Cold War era cannot be replicated, as the anti-industrial policy sentiment or the tide of "fair trade" against the promotion of industry or corporations is now working against the developing economies. Nations today are tightly bound by WTO rules and regulations, which arguably are not favorable to developmental industrial policy as I have already argued above. However, this point need not be overstressed, and nations need not be overly bound and discouraged by the socio-political environment and other conditions. Under whatever circumstances, the Korean lessons of keeping to economic discrimination principle in building economic institutions and policies as well as in creating the self-help spirit should not be ignored for those seeking economic development because this principle is the key to economic as well as human development by helping overcome the constraints of resource endowment and the international environment as well as developmental-unfriendly tradition and culture.

It may also be argued that Park's economic success based on the economic discrimination principle may have been possible because his political regime was authoritarian which in turn would have been helpful in keeping economic policies discriminatory. The implication is that in most advanced modern democracies, the Korean success model is not easily replicable. True to some extent is the possibility that enforcing economic discrimination may be easier under an authoritarian political regime than the modern advanced, Western style democracy, but here again this point should not be overstressed. Though the concept of democracy itself may be ambigious, any strong and persuasive leadership in a democratic regime or any bit of deviation from Western style democracy should not be identified automatically with de facto non-democracy, authoritarianism or even dictatorship. How to define the nature of the political leadership of the developmental state like that of Park Chung Hee, Lee Kwan Yew and others still remains controversial. Be that as it may, Park's success could not be attributed solely to his authoritarian political regime, as some dogmatic proponents of Western-stryle democracy had assumed, but mostly to his economic discriminatory leadership as has been discussed. In this regard, one should note that only a very few of many post-war authoritarian regimes or dictatorships around the world did in fact experience economic take-off. Moreover, it is also hard to find examples of developing economies that had experienced economic take-off under Western democratic regimes. From this observation, the twentieth century democracy, which arguably has leaned too much towards egalitarianism, does not seem to provide a good environment for economic development to take shape. That said however, the truth remains that only those countries that keep to the economic discrimination principle had any real chance to develop regardless of the type of political regimes; democracies, Western or any other styles, authoritarianism, dictatorships and any others. Now the choice is ours while here I present only the blueprint for the way forward towards the success.

In terms of the individual policies undertaken by Korea under Park's era for replication by latecomers, I would like to emphasize export promotion policy, corporate-promotional industrial policy, and rural development policy (Saemaul Undong), all under the economic discriminatory principle. Moreover, it is also worth remembering that any public policies, economic as well as social, should incorporate the nature of economic discrimination incentive structure if they are to mitigate moral hazard problems and instead help fill the national mindset with the self-help spirit and motivate its citizens to climb up the developmental ladder.

Hence, in sum, the key development principle that one can learn from our discussion of Korea's experiences is that economic discrimination is a necessary condition for development regardless of the kind of political regime and under any circumstances and at any time. Whether the national political leader(s) understands the significance of economic discrimination for development and has the will and determination to implement this principle remains a key factor for economic success as has been witnessed with the ED-leadership of Park Chung Hee. This is the most important lesson to be gained from Korea's economic development experiences not only for the developing economies, but also for the failing developed economies as well.

CHAPTER 9

Concluding Remarks

Abstract The concluding chapter consolidates the key lessons from Korea's experiences for development-seeking economies, whether developing and developed economies. The importance of economic discrimination and the warning of egalitarianism is again emphasized.

Keywords Economic discrimination · Warning of egalitarianism · Failing social policy · Discriminatory public policy

By way of concluding, I would like to consolidate the key lessons from Korea's experiences for development-seeking economies, not only for developing but also developed economies.

Economic development experiences have been so rare and uneven not only in the long history of humankind but also in the modern history of individual nations' transformation. From Korea's experiences, we learn two principles of economic development: First, a textbook description of market based on individual private property rights system and economic freedom, if not supplemented by private organization (corporation) and public organization (the government), has almost no chance in delivering economic development. There has always been a critical role of private corporations as well as the government for modern economic development. Private organizations are important as a positive factor to supplementing market failure (of market's economic discrimination

S.-H. Jwa, *The Rise and Fall of Korea's Economic Development*,
DOI 10.1007/978-3-319-58065-4_9

function) through exercising economic discrimination principle in management, and governments can and do also supplement the market by promoting the growth of private corporations and businesses activities through economic discrimination policies. The government's corporate-promotion policies have been the critical success factor for Korea's economic development. This strategy was highly discriminatory in the sense that the policy provided a differential incentive system based on the performances and treated different economic performances differently, by helping those who performed better than others. It is stated therefore that economic discrimination (ED) is a necessary condition for economic development.

Second, egalitarian policies tend to seriously mitigate economic differences artificially thereby working against economic dynamism and development since these policies dampen rather than strengthen the discrimination function of the market. Not only in Korea during the past 30 years but also in many other countries, developed and developing, the adoption of an egalitarian policy regime such as socialism, revised capitalism, social democracy and populist democracy have all experienced poor economic performances. It can therefore be said that economic egalitarianism is a sufficient condition for economic stagnation.

As concretely laid out in this book (and elsewhere), these two principles can be learned not only from Korea's economic success and mistakes, but also from the experiences of other nations across the world. These principles should be kept firmly in mind by latecomers when considering economic policy-making and when building economic institutions if they want to speed up the developmental process or, at least, would like to avoid some of the same mistakes committed by Korea in the recent past. The ideas in this book can be consolidated into a grand principle of economic development: "Economic discrimination is the necessary condition for economic development while economic egalitarianism is the sufficient condition for economic stagnation."[1] I hope that with this, I have provided a successful explanation for the reason why we observe a dichotomy in Korea's economic experiences between Park's regime and the era of mainstream thought as was raised at the end of Chap. 2.

At this point one may naturally feel curious about the implication of the new perspective of economic development on what to do about the economically underprivileged people. In this regard, the currently lingering question could be, "How to resolve the problem of unsustainability of most of the social empowerment policies mandated by the modern democracies", which has been vividly experienced by many economies, developing as well as developed, for the past few decades. I suggest that the economic discrimination principle can be a viable and effective solution. Economic discrimination can be a viable solution to the failing unsustainable social policy regime which is characterized by overwhelming egalitarianism and has not yet fully introduced any systematic incentive differentiation. The social empowerment policies which used to be and also tend to be egalitarian by nature are in general advised to adopt elements of economic discrimination to transform itself into a development policy. The economic development process needs to include those underprivileged people but it can only be done in a sustainable manner only with the application of economic discrimination in social as well as economic policy.

It is hoped that this book has effectively dismissed myths regarding Korea's economic development not only from empirical but also theoretical grounds. Particularly, concerning Park's political regime which has been much criticized as authoritarian and not development-friendly, it has been argued here that economic development has been and can be possible even without a fully-dressed democracy with market economy as long as economic discrimination is fully integrated into economic and social policy. A most recent example is witnessed in China's phenomenal growth over the last 30 years under a non-democratic, authoritarian political regime as argued in Jwa (2017) in which it is shown that China's policy embodies economic discrimination parallel to Park's economic development paradigm. More importantly, economic concentration to better performers, which is inevitably a result of the growth of better performing corporations and individuals, is a necessary outcome of economic development made possible by economic discrimination, without which economic development has been and is in fact impossible.

Moreover, according to the new theory of economic development used to interpret Korean economic experiences, industrial policy should not be considered an evil monster to be avoided, but rather should be a good addition to the list of government policy instruments and in particular if it is adopted as a corporate-promotion policy based on the market performances. This new interpretation of industrial policy may help increase the success probability of the policy even if it cannot guarantee success.

Furthermore, the corporate-led growth of the modern capitalist economy is in fact naturally a shared growth, while the socialist ideology led by Karl Marx has misinterpreted it as a mechanism for economic inequality per se. This is the reason why Park's corporate-led growth strategy based on economic discrimination turned out to be one of the best shared growth experiences. Unfortunately, it is also the reason why the anti-Park policy paradigm against corporate growth for the last 30 years has led to Korea's anti-shared growth stagnation. In this regard, Park's policy paradigm in adopting the economic discrimination principle is still in a sense a "living economics" from which the developing as well as the developed economies can find the keys to unlock the twin economic problems of stagnated growth and economic polarization.

Finally, any kind of public policies, if they are to be helpful for economic development, regardless of whether they aim to promote economic growth or social development, should take heed not to fall into the terrifying grip of the egalitarian trap stripping economic discrimination from the economy. Despite sometimes natural and popular tendency to disregard economic discrimination, we have shown that the Korean economic experience vividly demonstrates that economic discrimination cannot be sacrificed for economic development and prosperity.

Note

1. This principle has been proposed first by Jwa and Yoon (2004).

References

Jwa, Sung-Hee. 2017. *A General Theory of Economic Development: Towards A Capitalist Manifesto.* Cheltenham: Edward Elgar.

Jwa, Sung-Hee, and Yong Yoon. 2004. Political Institutions and Economic Development: A Study in Economic Discrimination and Political Philosophy. *Seoul Journal of Economics* 17 (3): 275–307.

Appendix

Appendix 1: Statistical data and figures

(1) Statistical data: Korean key economic indicators

Year	GDP (current $, billion)	GDP per capita (current $)	Real GDP growth (%)	CPI inflation (%)	M2 growth (%)	Current account balance (mil. $)	Gross savings rate	Gross investment rate	Gini coeff. (market income)
1955	1.4	64.0	5.8				8.2	11.7	
1956	1.4	65.0	0.7				6.5	8.3	
1957	1.7	73.0	9.2				11.9	14.3	
1958	1.9	80.0	6.5				9.7	11.5	
1959	2.0	81.0	5.4				8.3	10.1	
1960	2.0	79.0	2.3				8.1	9.7	
1961	2.2	84.0	6.9				10.7	11.7	
1962	2.4	90.0	3.8				10.1	13.1	
1963	2.8	103.0	9.2				13.8	17.8	
1964	3.0	106.0	9.5				13.5	14.7	
1965	3.1	108.0	7.2		51.9		12.5	14.0	
1966	3.8	128.0	12.0	11.3	51.5		16.2	20.6	
1967	4.4	145.0	9.1	10.9	61.3		15.6	21.1	
1968	5.4	174.0	13.2	10.7	72.0		18.1	25.9	
1969	6.8	216.0	14.5	12.4	54.7		21.0	28.8	
1970	8.2	253.0	10.0	16	24.9		18.4	25.7	
1971	9.5	290.0	10.5	13.5	29.3		15.6	25.2	
1972	10.8	324.0	7.2	11.7	33.6		17.5	21.2	
1973	13.8	406.0	14.8	3.2	36.1		22.9	25.7	
1974	19.5	562.0	9.5	24.3	21.5		22.2	32.3	
1975	21.7	615.0	7.9	25.2	25.2		19.5	29.1	

S.-H. Jwa, *The Rise and Fall of Korea's Economic Development*,
DOI 10.1007/978-3-319-58065-4

Year	GDP (current $, billion)	GDP per capita (current $)	Real GDP growth (%)	CPI infla-tion (%)	M2 growth (%)	Current account balance (mil. $)	Gross savings rate	Gross invest-ment rate	Gini coeff. (market income)
1976	29.8	831.0	13.1	15.3	35.1		25.1	27.5	
1977	38.3	1,051.0	12.3	10.1	40.1		28.6	30.6	
1978	53.7	1,452.0	10.8	14.5	35.4		31.3	34.2	
1979	64.3	1,713.0	8.6	18.3	29.7		30.6	38.0	
1980	64.9	1,703.0	−1.7	28.7	44.5	−6,845.0	25.4	34.6	
1981	72.4	1,870.0	7.2	21.4	36.1	−6,421.9	24.9	32.7	
1982	77.7	1,977.0	8.3	7.2	37.0	−5,542.1	26.8	32.3	
1983	87.0	2,179.0	13.2	3.4	22.9	−3,505.6	30.5	32.9	
1984	96.6	2,390.0	10.4	2.3	19.0	−1,755.8	32.6	32.5	
1985	100.2	2,456.0	7.7	2.5	18.1	−2,079.3	32.8	33.0	
1986	115.5	2,804.0	11.2	2.8	29.5	2,762.2	36.2	32.8	
1987	146.2	3,512.0	12.5	3	30.3	8,827.7	39.6	33.1	
1988	197.2	4,692.0	11.9	7.1	29.8	13,055.3	41.7	34.6	
1989	243.6	5,738.0	7.0	5.7	25.8	4,154.5	39.1	37.1	
1990	279.3	6,514.0	9.8	8.6	25.3	−2,403.6	39.3	39.5	0.266
1991	325.6	7,521.0	10.4	9.3	19.5	−7,604.6	39.3	41.4	0.259
1992	350.0	8,000.0	6.2	6.2	21.5	−2,431.7	38.4	38.5	0.254
1993	386.3	8,740.0	6.8	4.8	17.4	2,026.0	38.4	37.5	0.256
1994	455.5	10,204.0	9.2	6.3	21.1	−4,463.7	38.1	38.6	0.255
1995	556.3	12,337.0	9.6	4.5	23.3	−9,751.5	38.1	39.2	0.259
1996	597.9	13,133.0	7.6	4.9	16.7	−23,830.9	36.4	39.9	0.266
1997	557.6	12,134.0	5.9	4.4	19.7	−10,285.3	36.4	37.6	0.264
1998	374.9	8,100.0	−5.5	7.5	23.7	40,056.9	38.0	27.9	0.293
1999	485.0	10,404.0	11.3	0.8	5.1	21,608.2	35.9	31.2	0.298
2000	561.8	11,951.3	8.9	2.3	5.2	10,444.3	34.4	33.2	0.279
2001	533.1	11,254.3	4.5	4.1	8.1	2,700.2	32.4	31.9	0.290
2002	608.9	12,781.0	7.4	2.8	14.0	4,692.6	31.8	31.2	0.293
2003	680.4	14,206.1	2.9	3.5	3.0	11,877.4	33.3	32.3	0.283
2004	765.3	15,916.7	4.9	3.6	6.3	29,743.4	35.5	32.3	0.293
2005	898.0	18,636.0	3.9	2.8	7.0	12,654.8	33.8	32.5	0.298
2006	1,011.0	20,872.7	5.2	2.2	12.5	3,569.2	32.9	33.0	0.305
2007	1,122.7	23,062.1	5.5	2.5	10.8	11,794.5	33.2	32.8	0.316
2008	1,001.7	20,420.6	2.8	4.7	12.0	3,189.7	32.9	33.0	0.319
2009	902.3	18,299.5	0.7	2.8	9.9	33,593.3	32.9	28.6	0.320
2010	1,094.3	22,083.2	6.5	2.9	6.0	28,850.4	35.0	32.1	0.315
2011	1,202.7	24,083.7	3.7	4	5.5	18,655.8	34.6	32.9	0.313
2012	1,222.4	24,349.9	2.3	2.2	4.8	50,835.0	34.2	30.8	0.310
2013	1,305.4	25,885.6	2.9	1.3	4.6	81,148.2	34.3	29.0	0.307
2014	1,411.0	27,804.5	3.3	1.3	8.1	84,373.0	34.5	29.3	0.308
2015	1,382.4	27,097.1	2.6	0.7	8.2	105,870.7	35.4	28.5	0.305

Source The Bank of Korea

Per capita Corporate Asset

Year	1968	1969	1970	1971	1972	1973	1974	1975	1976
Per capita Corporate Assets(Won), (Growth rate, %)	77,356	121,981 (57.7)	160,714 (31.8)	201,719 (25.5)	249,298 (23.6)	303,629 (21.8)	430,467 (41.8)	610,822 (41.9)	877,903 (43.7)

Year	1977	1978	1979	1980	1981	1982	1983	1984	1985
Per capita Corporate Assets(Won), (Growth rate, %)	1,294,864 (47.5)	2,083,192 (60.9)	2,787,001 (33.8)	3,949,779 (41.7)	5,098,036 (29.1)	6,122,519 (20.1)	7,079,229 (15.6)	7,986,241 (12.8)	9,219,242 (15.4)

Year	1986	1987	1988	1989	1990	1991	1992	1993
Per capita Corporate Assets(Won), (Growth rate, %)	9,796,480 (6.3)	10,598,788 (8.2)	11,587,632 (9.3)	14,115,570 (21.8)	18,124,864 (28.4)	22,864,598 (26.2)	26,112,071 (14.2)	29,704,619 (13.8)

Year	1994	1995	1996	1997	1998	1999	2000	2001
Per capita Corporate Assets(Won), (Growth rate, %)	35,910,485 (20.9)	43,693,761 (21.7)	49,801,027 (14.0)	23,068,716 (−53.7)	23,650,369 (2.5)	24,717,398 (4.5)	24,461,402 (−1.0)	24,067,473 (−1.6)

Year	2002	2003	2004	2005	2006	2007	2008	2009
Per capita Corporate Assets(Won), (Growth rate, %)	24,937,118 (3.6)	26,261,640 (5.3)	27,961,929 (6.5)	30,342,062 (8.5)	32,783,126 (8.0)	36,684,187 (11.9)	42,712,792 (16.4)	46,146,124 (8.0)

Year	2010	2011	2012	2013	2014	2015
Per capita Corporate Assets(Won), (Growth rate, %)	50,380,393 (9.2)	54,807,600 (8.8)	57,327,228 (4.6)	59,700,662 (4.1)	62,009,928 (3.9)	64,779,043 (4.5)

Source Author's calculation based on "Corporate Management Analysis", The Bank of Korea

<Sectoral real GDP ratio>
Unit: %

Year	1955	1956	1957	1958	1959	1960	1961	1962	1963	1964	1965	1966	1967	1968	1969
Agriculture/Fishery	30.1	28.2	28.3	28.8	27.3	26.3	28.3	25.5	25.7	27.3	25.7	25.0	21.7	19.2	18.3
Manufacturing	3.4	3.9	3.9	4.1	4.2	4.4	4.4	4.9	5.2	5.2	5.9	6.3	7.1	7.7	7.9
Construction	4.3	3.9	4.5	4.3	5.0	4.8	4.9	5.4	5.8	5.6	6.5	7.0	7.7	9.4	11.3
Services and others	62.2	63.9	63.3	62.8	63.4	64.4	62.4	64.2	63.3	62.0	61.9	61.7	63.5	63.7	62.4
GDP	100.0	100.0	100.0	100.0	100.0	100.0	100.0	100.0	100.0	100.0	100.0	100.0	100.0	100.0	100.0

Year	1970	1971	1972	1973	1974	1975	1976	1977	1978	1979	1980	1981	1982	1983	1984
Agriculture/ Fishery	16.5	15.8	15.2	14.1	13.7	13.3	12.8	11.8	9.6	9.8	8.3	9.0	9.0	8.6	7.6
Manufac- turing	8.4	8.9	9.5	10.8	11.5	12.1	12.9	13.3	15.0	15.2	15.2	15.5	15.0	15.5	16.8
Construction	10.7	9.5	8.7	9.3	9.5	9.3	9.0	10.2	11.8	11.4	11.3	9.8	10.4	11.1	10.6
Services and others	64.4	65.8	66.6	65.8	65.4	65.3	65.3	64.6	63.6	63.5	65.2	65.7	65.7	64.7	64.9
GDP	100.0	100.0	100.0	100.0	100.0	100.0	100.0	100.0	100.0	100.0	100.0	100.0	100.0	100.0	100.0

Year	1985	1986	1987	1988	1989	1990	1991	1992	1993	1994	1995	1996	1997	1998	1999
Agriculture/ Fishery	7.5	7.1	6.0	5.9	5.5	4.7	4.4	4.5	4.1	3.7	3.6	3.5	3.5	3.4	3.2
Manufacturing	16.7	17.4	18.6	18.8	18.3	18.6	18.9	18.9	18.9	19.3	19.9	20.0	20.0	19.5	21.3
Construction	10.4	9.7	9.5	9.1	9.6	10.8	10.9	10.1	10.3	9.8	9.4	9.3	8.9	8.3	6.9
Services and others	65.4	65.8	65.9	66.2	66.6	65.9	65.8	66.5	66.8	67.1	67.0	67.1	67.6	68.7	68.5
GDP	100.0	100.0	100.0	100.0	100.0	100.0	100.0	100.0	100.0	100.0	100.0	100.0	100.0	100.0	100.0

Year	2000	2001	2002	2003	2004	2005	2006	2007	2008	2009	2010	2011	2012	2013	2014	2015
Agriculture/ Fishery	3.0	2.9	2.7	2.4	2.5	2.5	2.4	2.4	2.4	2.5	2.2	2.1	2.0	2.1	2.1	2.0
Manufacturing	22.7	22.5	22.8	23.3	24.4	24.8	25.4	26.1	26.4	26.0	27.8	28.6	28.6	28.8	28.8	28.5
Construction	6.1	6.1	5.8	6.1	5.9	5.7	5.5	5.3	5.0	5.1	4.6	4.2	4.1	4.1	4.0	4.0
Services and others	68.2	68.5	68.7	68.1	67.2	67.0	66.7	66.2	66.2	66.3	65.3	65.1	65.3	65.1	65.1	65.6
GDP	100.0	100.0	100.0	100.0	100.0	100.0	100.0	100.0	100.0	100.0	100.0	100.0	100.0	100.0	100.0	100.0

Source The Bank of Korea

(2) Figures of key economic indicators

Real GDP

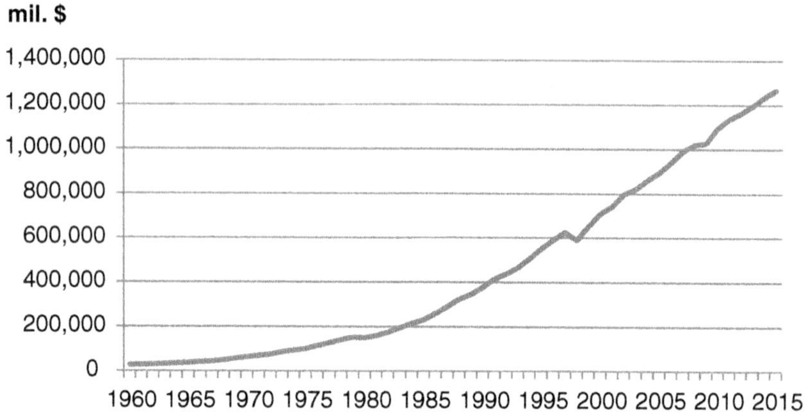

Note 2010 dollar base. *Source* The World Bank

Real per capita GDP

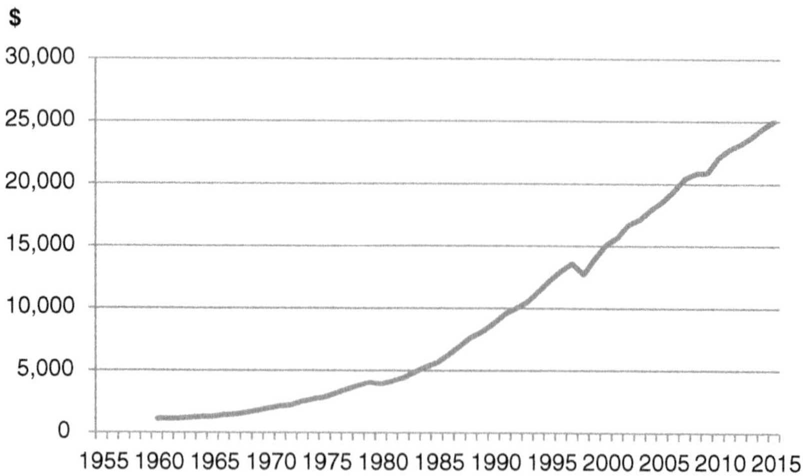

Note 2010 dollar base. *Source* The World Bank

South and North Korea real GDP comparison

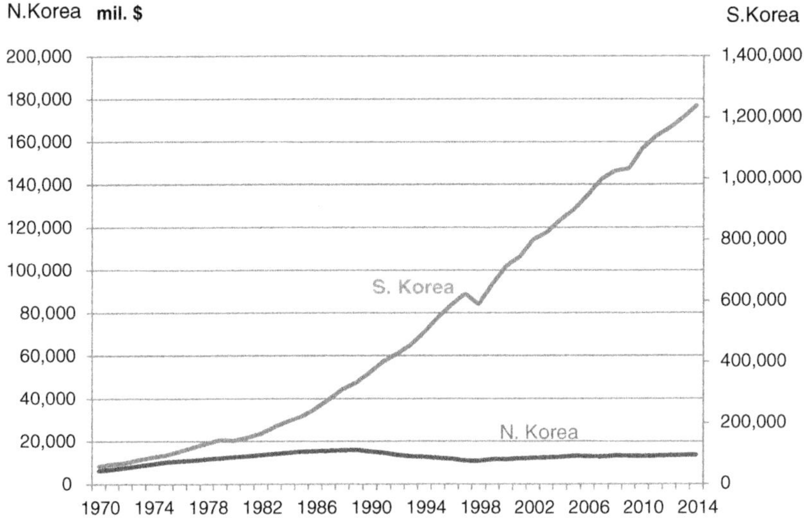

Note 2005 dollar base. *Source* UN

Real GDP growth (annual)

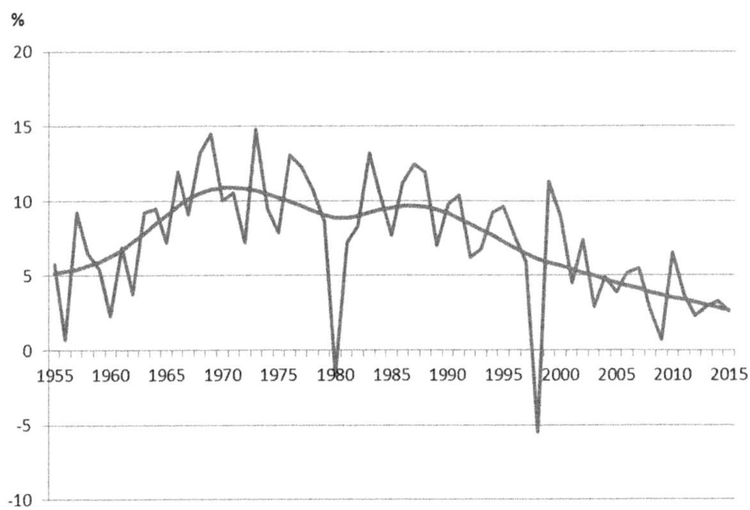

Note: *Blue* actual growth rate, *red* growth trend by Hoddrick-Prescott filter (Color figure online). *Source* The Bank of Korea

CPI inflation (annual)

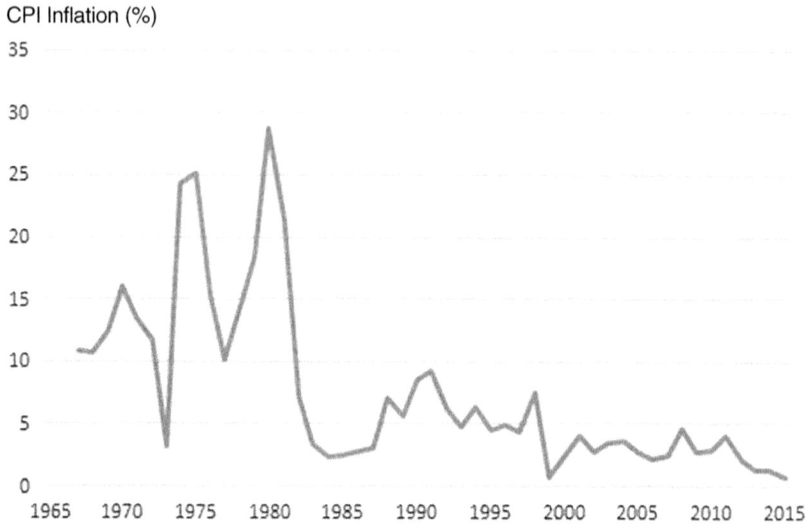

Source The Bank of Korea

Money (M2) growth (annual)

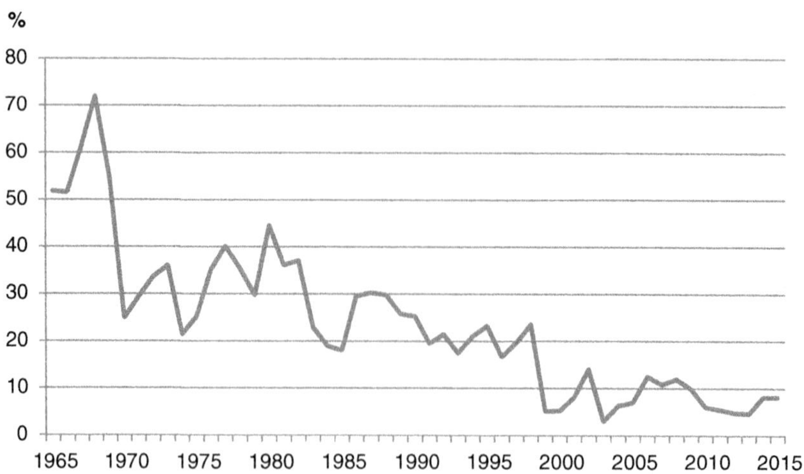

Source The Bank of Korea

Won/Dollar exchange rate (at the end of period)

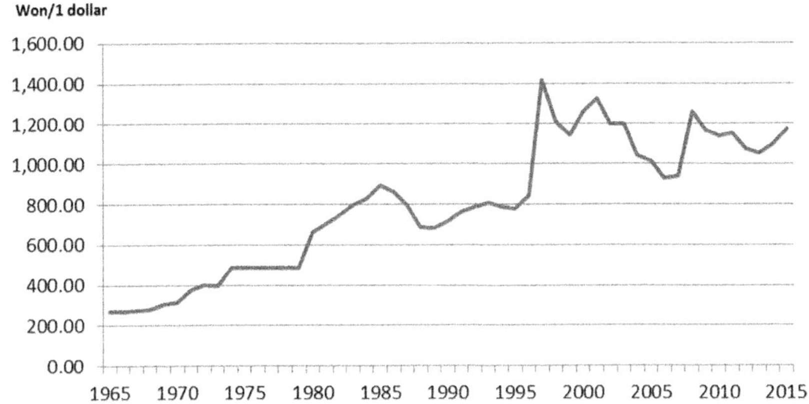

Source The Bank of Korea

Current account balance

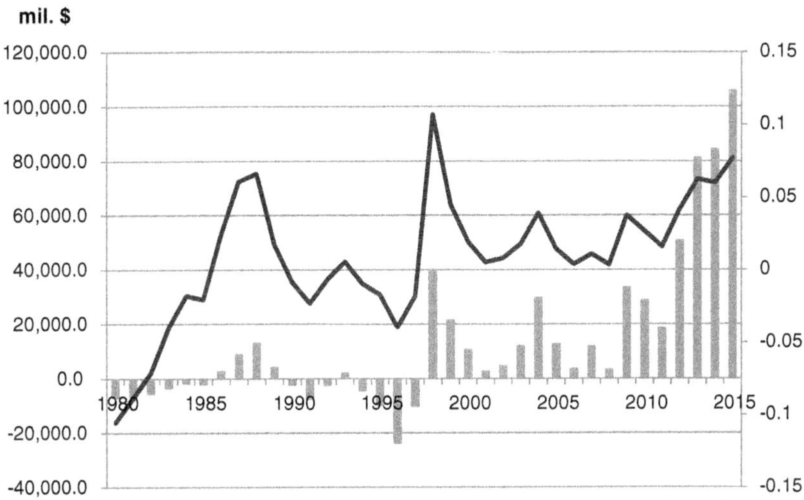

Note CA/GDP (*red*, right axis), CA (*blue*, left axis) (Color figure online). *Source* The Bank of Korea

Growth rate of import and export

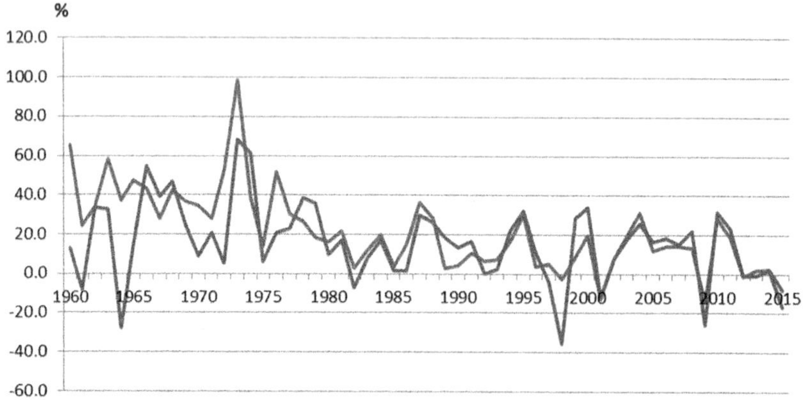

Note: *Blue* import, *red* export (Color figure online). *Source* The Bank of Korea

Gross savings rate

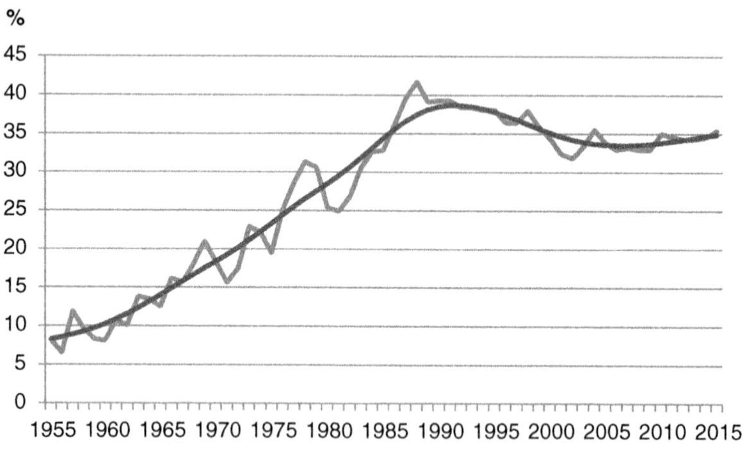

Note: *Blue* actual growth rate, *red* growth trend by Hoddrick-Prescott filter (Color figure online). *Source* The Bank of Korea

Household sector gross savings rate

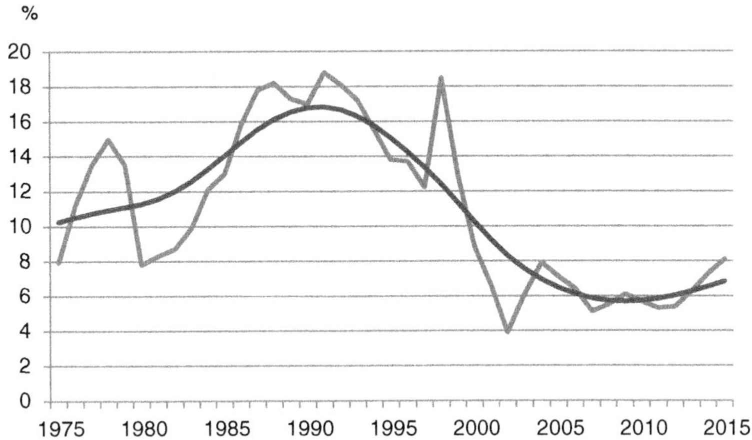

Note: *Blue* actual growth rate, *red* growth trend by Hoddrick-Prescott filter (Color figure online). *Source* The Bank of Korea

Corporate sector gross savings rate

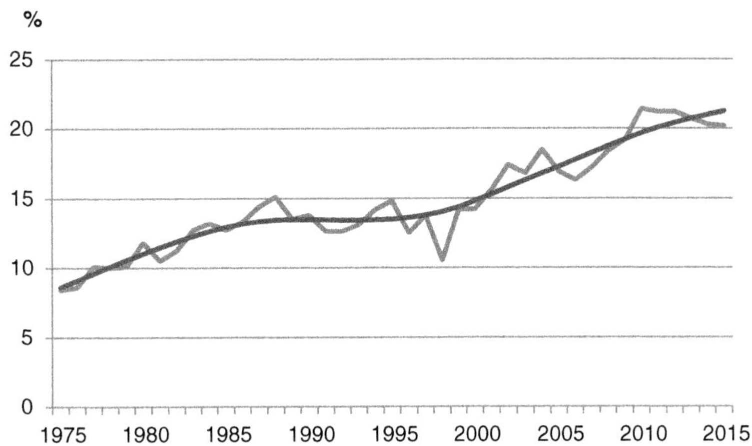

Note: *Blue* actual growth rate, *red* growth trend by Hoddrick-Prescott filter (Color figure online). *Source* The Bank of Korea

Gross investment rate

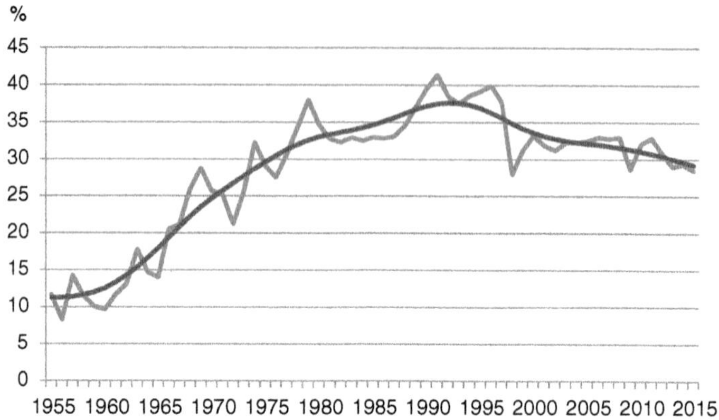

Note: *Blue* actual growth rate, *red* growth trend by Hoddrick-Prescott filter (Color figure online). *Source* The Bank of Korea

Growth rate of total number of the employed

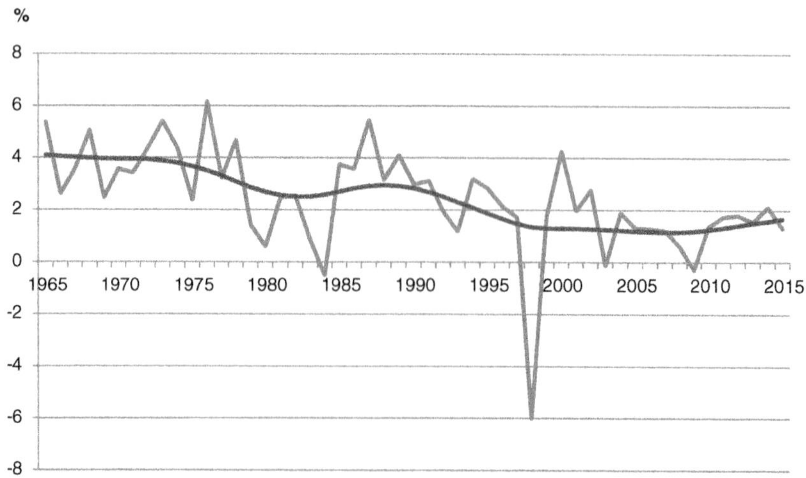

Note: *Blue* actual growth rate, *red* growth trend by Hoddrick-Prescott filter (Color figure online). *Source* The Bank of Korea

Gini coefficient

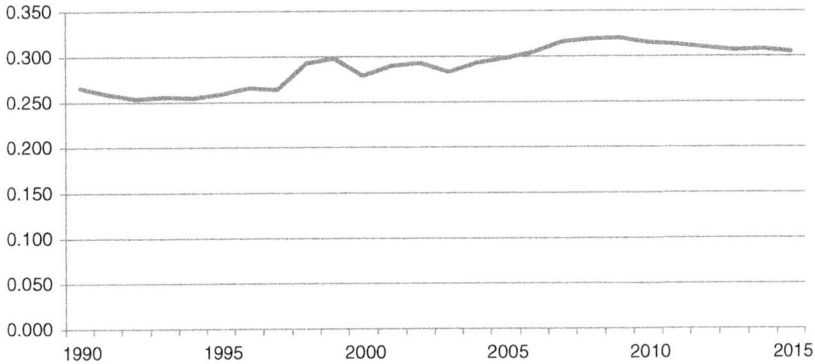

Note Urban household market income. *Source* The Bank of Korea

Number of corporations with the employees above 500

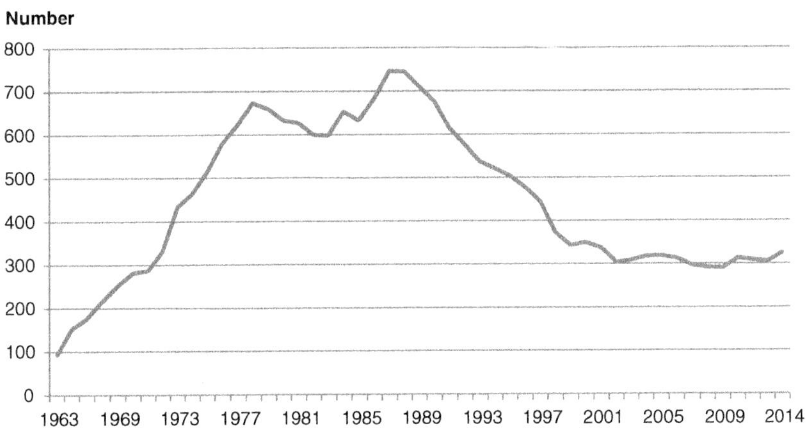

Note Number of business establishments. *Source* Statistics Korea

Number of corporations with the employees between 300–499

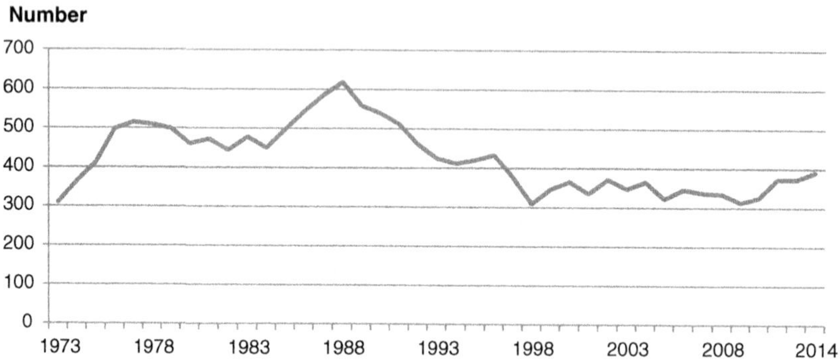

Note Number of business establishments. *Source* Statistics Korea

Number of corporations with the employees below 300

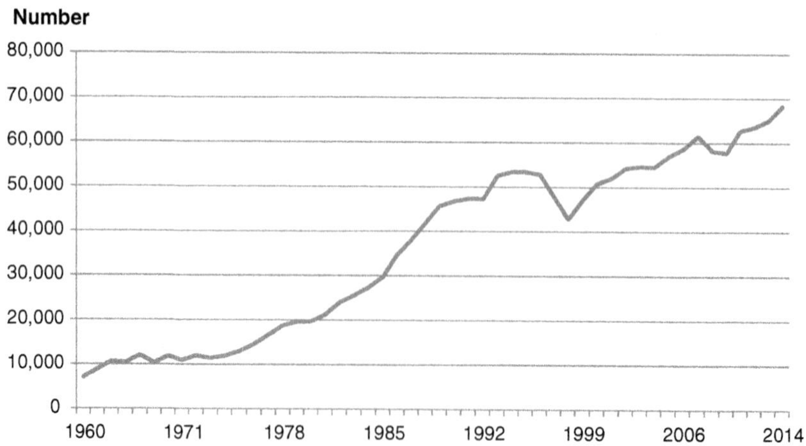

Note Number of business establishments. *Source* Statistics Korea

Per capita corporate assets

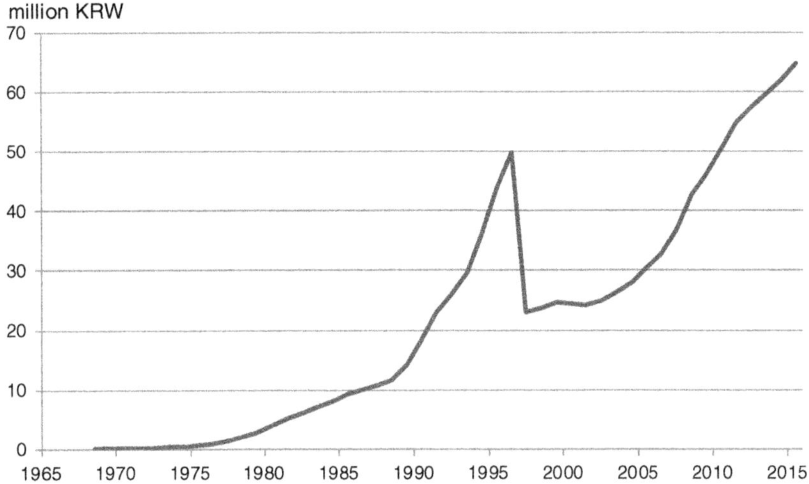

Note Korea's total corporate assets/total population. *Source* Author's calculation based on "Corporate Management Analysis", The Bank of Korea

Growth rate of per capita corporate assets

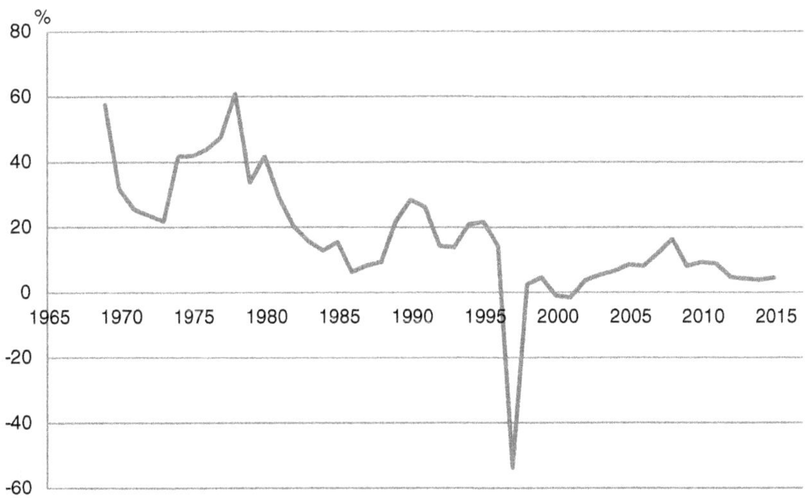

Note Korea's total corporate assets/total population. *Source* Author's calculation based on "Corporate Management Analysis", The Bank of Korea

Appendix 2: Chronology of major events (1945–2016)

1945 August: After the surrender of Japan, the Korean peninsula is divided between Soviet and American occupation forces at the 38th parallel.

1948 May: UN sponsored elections are held in South Korea.
August: Establishment of the Republic of Korea with Syngman Rhee as the first President.
September: Establishment of the Democratic People's Republic of Korea with Kim Il-sung as Premier.

1950 June 25: The Korean War begins.

1953 July: The Korean War is halted by the Korean Armistice Agreement that has remained in force until now.

1960 A student uprising begins the April Revolution which overthrows the autocratic First Republic of South Korea. Syngman Rhee resigns and goes into exile.

1961 May: Military forces, headed by General Park Chung Hee, overthrow the Second Republic of South Korea in what is known as the Revolution or the Military Coup d'état of 16 May.
July: Enact of anticommunism law.
November: Summit conference for normalization of Korea–Japanese relations.
July: Establishment of EPB (Economic Planning Board).
November: Park Chung Hee's official visit to the United States of America.

1962 Start of the first 5-year plans of South Korea.
March: Enactment of 16 Acts including Export Promotion Law.
June: The Second Monetary Reform.
June: Establishment KOTRA (Korea Trade Promotion Agency).

1963 November: President Park Chung Hee visited the US to attend President Kennedy funeral ceremony and had a summit meeting with US President Lyndon B. Johnson.
December: Park Chung Hee inaugurated as the 5th President and the Third Republic starts.
December: One hundred and twenty three (123) mining workers headed towards West Germany.

1964 May: Devaluation of Korean Currency to 255 Won per US dollar.
August: Establishment of Korea Export Industrial Corporation.

November: Celebrate 100 million US dollar export performance. November 31 of every year began to be designated as "the export day."

1965 May: President Park Chung Hee visited the US and had a summit meeting with President Lyndon B. Johnson.
June: Signing of Treaty on Basic Relations between Japan and the Republic of Korea. Receiving indemnities for Japan's colonization as well as commercial loans. Earned both much controversy and procurement of budgets for later economic developments.
July: Dispatch of Korean combat troops to Vietnam.

1966 February: Establishment of KIST (Korea Institute of Science and Technology).
October: US President Lyndon B. Johnson visited Korea and had a summit meeting with President Park Chung Hee.

1967 Start of the second 5-year plans of South Korea.
April: Korea becomes a member of GATT.
July: Park Chung Hee took office as the 6th President of Korea.

1968 April: Establishment of the Pohang Iron and Steel Company (POSCO).

1970 April: Start of the government-operated Saemaul Undong (New Village Movement).
July: Gyeongbu Expressway is completed and opened to traffic.
December: Korea export recorded more than $1 billion.

1971 July: Park Chung Hee took office as the 7th President.

1972 Start of the third 5-year plans of South Korea.
December: Park Chung Hee took office as the 8th President.

1973 January: President Park declared Heavy and Chemical Industrialization (HCI) policy.

1977 Start of the fourth 5-year plans of South Korea.
December: Celebration of achievement of 10 billion dollars gained by exports.

1978 December: Park Chung Hee took office as the 9th President.

1979 October: President Park assassinated by the head of the Korean Central Intelligence Agency. Second oil crisis begins.

1980 January: New economy policy shifts emphasis away from economic growth to a concern about economic stability and equity.
October: World-wide poor harvest and food shortage hit the Korean economy.

1981	January: Democratic Justice Party formed. March: Chun Doo-hwan inaugurated as the 12th President and the Fifth Republic begins. August: Liberalization of foreign trade begins.
1982	January: 37-year-old nightly curfew lifted.
1983	July: Korean population reaches 40 million. September: Korean airliner shot down by USSR after straying off course.
1984	September: President Chun's state visit to Japan. Establishment of Korea Investment Fund in Korean stock market.
1985	January: 'Three lows'—low oil price, low interest rates, and low dollar and Korean won value vis-a-vis Japanese Yen—spurs export boom.
1986	September: Asian Games held in Seoul. November: Exports exceed imports for the first time since the First 5-Year Economic Development Plan began. December: Savings exceed investment for the first time since the First 5-Year Plan began.
1987	June 29: Democratization declaration by ruling party Presidential candidate Roh Tae-woo. August: Labor disputes broke out nation-wide.
1988	February: Roh Tae-woo inaugurated as the 13th President and the Sixth Republic begins. July: Iran–Iraq War ends. Policy of limiting real estate transactions announced. October: Policy of opening up trade with North Korea announced. September–October: 1988 Summer Olympics held in Seoul.
1989	April: Plan for the construction of new cities (2 million housing project) announced.
1990	September: South Korea and the USSR establish diplomatic relations.
1991	September: South Korea (ROK) and North Korea (DPRK) join the United Nations (UN).
1992	January: The Korean stocks are opened to foreign investors. August: South Korea and the People's Republic of China (PRC) establish diplomatic relations.
1993	February: Kim Young-Sam inaugurated as the 14th President. August: The new real name financial transaction begins.

1994 July: Kim Jong-il takes control of North Korea upon the death of his father Kim Il-sung.

1995 January: WTO (World Trade Organization) begins.
July: The rice aids to North Korea begins.
Per capita income surpasses US$10,000

1996 December: Korea becomes a member of OECD

1997 January: Hanbo Steel (15th largest chaebol) files for bankruptcy.
April: Jinro Group (19th largest chaebol) files for bankruptcy.
May: The Daenong Group files for bankruptcy.
July: Kia Motors files for bankruptcy.
October: Standard & Poor's downgrades Korea's sovereign-credit ratings from AA– to A+ (long-term) and A1+ to A1 (short-term).
November 21: The Ministry of Finance and Economy (MOFE) announces the decision to seek a rescue package from the IMF.
November 26: Standard & Poor's downgrades Korea's sovereign credit ratings from A+ to A– (long-term) and from A1 to A2 (short-term).
December 10: Moody's downgrades Korea's sovereign-credit ratings to junk-bond status, from A3 to Baa2 (long-term) and P3 to NP (short-term).
December 11: The stock-investment limit for foreigners is increased to 50%. Standard & Poor's downgrades Korea's sovereign credit ratings from A– to BBB–.
December 12: To stabilize financial markets, the Bank of Korea (BOK) announces W7.3 trillion to fund 14 merchant banks, raises the limit for foreign ownership to corporate bonds of conglomerates from 10 to 30%, raises the limit on non-guaranteed convertible bonds and convertible-bond investment of conglomerates from 30 to 50%, and abolishes the limits on non-guaranteed corporate bonds and convertible bonds of SMEs.
December 16: The legal interest-rate ceiling is raised from 25 to 40%. A timetable is established for the opening of the short-term financial market by February 1998. The limit for foreign investment in financial institutions is raised.
December 18: Kim Dae-jung elected as the 15th President.
December 21: Moody's downgrades Korea's sovereign credit ratings for long-term debt to Baa2 (junk bond).

December 23: The selling rate for US$ 1 cash breaks the Won 2,000. Standard & Poor's downgrades Korea's sovereign credit ratings from BBB– to B+. Limits on investment on corporate bonds are abolished. Foreign participation in government-bond investments is approved, with a limit of 30% per item.
December 30: The IMF provides US$ 2 billion of early support funds (third disbursement). All limits on foreign investment in long and short-term corporate and government bonds are lifted.

1998 January: Kim Dae-jung asks chairmen of the four largest business groups to restructure chaebols.
February: Kim Dae-jung is inaugurated as the 15th President.
April: Financial Supervisory Committee established.
September: Federation of Korean Industries agreed to exchange business among groups under the Big Deal Agreement.
December: Government and five business groups sign agreements on the Big Deal.

1999 January: Euro, the single European currency, comes into effect. Financial Supervisory Board established.
April: Korea Futures Market opens.
The second largest chaebol—Daewoo collapsed, resulting in the largest corporate bankruptcy in modern history.

2000 June: Summit in Pyongyang between Kim Jong-il and South Korean President Kim Dae-jung.
July: World Bank Office in Seoul closed.

2001 March: Inchon Airport opens.
August: Repayment of IMF loans 3 years ahead of schedule, and economic sovereignty regained.
September: The US 9/11 terrorist attacks on World Trade Center and Pentagon building.
October: The US-Afghanistan war against terrorism begins.

2002 The 2002 FIFA World Cup jointly held by Korea and Japan.
June: North Korean warship fired against South Korea warship at the Yellow Sea.

2003 February: Roh Moo-hyun inaugurated as the 16th president.

2004 April: South Korea's first free trade agreement, Korea-Chile FTA enters into force.

2007 October: The second summit between DPRK and ROK leaders is held, with Roh Moo-hyun representing the south and Kim Jong-il the north.

December: Conservative former Hyundai CEO Lee Myung-Bak wins landslide victory in presidential election
Per capita income surpasses US$20,000.

2008 February: Lee Myung-Bak inaugurated as the 17th President.
October: South Korean banks become vulnerable to global credit crisis as result of having taken on high levels of foreign debt. Government announces $130 bn financial rescue package to shore up banking system and stabilize markets in the wake of the US subprime mortgage crisis.

2009 February: South Korea's central bank cuts interest rates to a record low, amid forecasts that the economy is likely to suffer its first annual contraction for more than 10 years.

2010 March: A South Korea warship, the Cheonan sank into deep sea by the North Korea Navy attack.
October: North Korea artillery hit Yeonpyeong Island and killed 2 soldiers and 2 civilians.
December: Korea's total trade volume surpassed 1 trillion dollars for the first time in history.

2011 July: Korea–European Union Free Trade Agreement enters into force.
December: Kim Jong-il dies, and his son Kim Jong-un takes over as the Supreme Leader of North Korea.

2012 March: Korea–US Free Trade Agreement (KORUS FTA) enters into force.

2013 February: Park Geun-Hye, daughter of late President Park Chung Hee, began serving as South Korea's first female and the 18th president of South Korea.

2014 November: Korea–China Free Trade Agreement (KORUS FTA) enters into force.

2016 February: South Korea shut off Kaesong Industrial Complex located at North Korean region.
June: The U.S. forces in Korea has decided to deploy a battery of the Terminal High Altitude Area Defense (THAAD) weapon system at South Korea region.
October: The bizarre political scandal led to an impeachment move against President Park Geun-Hye.
November: The Nation Assembly passed presidential impeachment motion and stopped president's power.

2017 March 10: President Park Geun-Hye is impeached.
May, 9: Moon Jae-In becomes the 19th President.

Index

S.-H. Jwa, *The Rise and Fall of Korea's Economic Development*,
DOI 10.1007/978-3-319-58065-4

E

F

Printed by Printforce, the Netherlands